Do You Ever Cry, Dad?

Do You Ever Ever Cry, Dad?

A Father's Guide
to Surviving
Family Breakup

I.J. Schecter

DUNDURN
TORONTO

Cover image: istock.com/486417825
Printer: Webcom, a division of Marquis Book Printing Inc.

Library and Archives Canada Cataloguing in Publication

Schecter, I. J., 1971-, author
   Do you ever cry, dad? : a father's guide to surviving family
breakup / I.J. Schecter.

Issued in print and electronic formats.
ISBN 978-1-4597-4267-3 (softcover).--ISBN 978-1-4597-4268-0 (PDF).--
ISBN 978-1-4597-4269-7 (EPUB)

   1. Divorced fathers. 2. Father and child. I. Title.

HQ756.S34 2019   306.874'2   C2018-905370-4
                                           C2018-905371-2

1 2 3 4 5   23 22 21 20 19

Conseil des Arts du Canada   Canada Council for the Arts

ONTARIO ARTS COUNCIL
CONSEIL DES ARTS DE L'ONTARIO
an Ontario government agency
un organisme du gouvernement de l'Ontario

We acknowledge the support of the **Canada Council for the Arts**, which last year invested $153 million to bring the arts to Canadians throughout the country, and the **Ontario Arts Council** for our publishing program. We also acknowledge the financial support of the **Government of Ontario**, through the **Ontario Book Publishing Tax Credit** and **Ontario Creates**, and the **Government of Canada**.

Nous remercions le **Conseil des arts du Canada** de son soutien. L'an dernier, le Conseil a investi 153 millions de dollars pour mettre de l'art dans la vie des Canadiennes et des Canadiens de tout le pays.

Care has been taken to trace the ownership of copyright material used in this book. The author and the publisher welcome any information enabling them to rectify any references or credits in subsequent editions.
                                                    — J. Kirk Howard, President

The publisher is not responsible for websites or their content unless they are owned by the publisher.

Printed and bound in Canada.

VISIT US AT

  dundurn.com | @dundurnpress | dundurnpress | dundurnpress

Dundurn
3 Church Street, Suite 500
Toronto, Ontario, Canada
M5E 1M2

To my parents, for their unending comfort and shelter
To my sister, for her daily reminders and reassurance
To my kids, for being the best part of me
To Fulvia, for her bottomless love

Contents

Introduction

I have written about many subjects in my career, from golf to nudism (though never together — that would have been interesting). Most writers agree that one of the best parts of the job is the opportunity to learn about so many different subjects. Recently I've had to learn about a topic I didn't see coming: how to be a divorced dad. What I've learned is that for the most part, in this area, you're making guesses. With the help of time, and the caring and wisdom of others, you get a little better at making those guesses, but there's no formula for success. Every situation is different — every kid, every dad, every ex, every family — so the best you can do is the best you can do.

I wish I could count the number of bad guesses I've made on one hand, but the truth is, as for most split dads, the list of my poor guesses is longer than the list of Wayne Gretzky's records. Most experts tend to agree on certain common-sense principles that can guide your behaviour, but the rest is kind of a crapshoot. The purpose of this book is to help you, and other dads, make the best guesses you can, based on my experience, the experiences of others, and the views of professionals. I want to assure you that, even when those guesses aren't necessarily right, the ramifications aren't as bad or as long-term as you fear, as long as your children know you love them and are around to stay. I want to invite you into a community of dads who have gone through, or are going through, many of the same things you are. And, perhaps most of all, I want to let you know that things will get better.

――――――

In the first year after my split, I encountered two individuals whom I now think of as my guardian angels. Both were police officers. I met them eight months apart.

The first meeting occurred about three months after my ex and I told our three kids we were breaking up, which was, needless to say, the worst moment of my life. At that point I was, to put it mildly, a complete mess. I'd been attempting to manage the few parts of my life I felt I could control: the quality of my work, the state of my body, the way I treated others. But those were the things on the outside. The part inside, my heart, well, I had only so much control over that, and the pain it was trying to contain was overwhelming.

I had just spent the evening with Dustin, Cory, and Alisha,* then dropped them back "home" with their mom and drove away. It hurts to even write "drove away." Those words make me want to cry, as do any words that describe the action of physically leaving my kids. Typically, after parting ways, I would drive a few blocks, pull over, and cry. Those tears expressed a lot of complicated emotions, but mostly just unmitigated pain. Often I would think about when my kids were born: the pure love and instinctive connection I'd felt. What I was experiencing after the breakup felt in many ways opposite — the emptiness of saying goodbye to them, the feeling of detachment instead of connection. The first time I had to leave them after the split, I felt like the pain might kill me.

At some point after stopping the car, I would pull myself together and drive back "home" (my parents' apartment). Then I would try to do something productive: exercise, write, correspond with people important to me, read, spend time talking to my mom and dad. On this particular evening, after the cry had exhausted itself and I started driving home,

――――――

* For their privacy, I have changed my kids' names.

almost immediately I saw flashing lights in my rear-view mirror. I pulled over impassively. The cop, an older guy who looked like he'd been on the force for a long time — thinning hairline, gray at the temples, bit of a paunch — walked toward me and I lowered the window, getting ready to hand over my licence and registration. He was in cop mode, serious and authoritative, flipping open his pad and clicking his pen.

When he looked up and saw my face, he paused for a long moment. I was holding out my documents, but he didn't take them. He seemed frozen, as though he wasn't looking at a person, but a ghost. After what felt like a long time, he spoke. "Sir," he said, in a quiet voice, "I don't know what's happening in your life right now, but I need you to do something. I need you to promise me you're going to drive home, and then I need you to promise me you aren't going to get behind the wheel again when you feel like this. This is a school zone, sir, and you were going fast enough to do something really dangerous. Do you understand what I'm saying to you?" He was speaking very slowly and carefully. "Sir?"

"Um, yes," I said. "Sorry. Yes. Thank you."

"Do you want to wait a while, or do you feel you're okay to drive home?"

"I'm okay," I said.

"All right," he said. "Straight home, then."

I saw my hand go out and grasp his. I heard myself say something about his being a good cop, or maybe a good man. While he walked back to his cruiser, I tilted down the mirror to look at myself. What I saw reminded me of a day soon after Dustin was born, when I'd gone into work feeling exhausted, but thinking I could fool people for one day. Ten minutes in, someone had walked by, done a double take, and said to me, "Wow, you look *so* tired." We can fool people sometimes, but not when the fatigue, or the pain, is blindingly obvious to them (even if it may not be to us). Now, looking at myself in the rear-view, I was stunned at how I looked. Maybe the best way to say it is I was there, but barely looked like I was. I am forever grateful to that cop not only for his humanity, but also for alerting me to the fact that I was in a far worse state than I'd recognized.

Eight months later, after having again said good night to my kids, again detesting the moment of walking away, again feeling despair at not seeing them in their pyjamas in the morning, I was driving down the same street as before. Again I saw flashing lights and heard a siren. This time I felt the same righteous indignation most of us feel in such a moment (right before you start to admit you might have actually done something wrong). This time as the cop approached my door, I didn't reach for my licence and registration, because I remembered what had happened before and assumed it would happen again. I even worked to achieve the same kind of look of desolation I'd had the previous time, just to make sure I would get out of this ticket too.

The officer, younger and more trim than the one who had pulled me over months before, looked at me and asked for my documents. Nothing in his demeanour changed; he started cop and stayed cop. I told him I was going through a split and having a rough day. He said, "I understand. Licence and registration, please." I hadn't been going very fast this time — just fast enough to merit a ticket. But if there was ever a positive ticket to get, this was it. Because what this cop saw was a man who was present, aware, and, all other things being equal, normal. What the other cop had seen was a man hardly there, obliviously driving a two-ton weapon through a school zone.

Some eleven months after my breakup, I was still in tremendous pain. I was still burdened by a sorrow I'd never known, still just trying to, as Tom Hanks's widower character Sam Baldwin puts it in the movie *Sleepless in Seattle*, "get out of bed every morning, breathe in and out all day long." But that ticket, although aggravating in the way any ticket is, was also the first sign that things might get better.

In the months before, during, and after my split, I'd spoken to dozens of friends and others who had gone through divorce, either as the parents doing the splitting or as the children of those parents. They'd all had useful and compassionate things to say. But the advice of one person stood out, and it was those words I thought about as I drove away, ticket in hand. He'd said, "Look, I.J., there's no way to make it go faster or make it hurt less. But eventually, it changes. It's bad, it's bad, it's bad, and then one day, it's good." What I was feeling by then, nearly a year in, couldn't have been remotely described as "good," but the fact that the second cop recognized me as a person conscious enough to deserve the ticket signalled that I was starting to come back into myself, even if only a tiny bit. I still found it a monumental effort to remain functional and positive from one day to the next, but at least I was starting to reawaken.

Those two men were my guardian angels because they represented two essential parts of my journey: the pain that cannot be bypassed or rushed, and the first small moments that indicate things might be okay, if not today, then maybe tomorrow. The first angel let me know that I was in a really dark place and not entirely aware of my actions. The second let me know that I was starting to become whole again.

Before, between, and since these two encounters, my kids have gone through a bracing series of ups and downs, each in their own way and according to their personality. During their collective and individual passages, certain moments have made me want to cry, scream, or both. There was the time, just weeks after the split, when I tried to do something normal: take them tobogganing. Rather than being a fun event, this ended up instead with everyone's tension spilling over, me yelling insanely at the winter sky, and the kids looking on horrified as though I was going crazy, which I pretty much was. There was the moment when I walked into Dustin's room one evening to find all of the poems and stories I had written for him over ten years torn apart and littering his floor. There was the bedtime cuddle with Alisha when I thought she had fallen asleep on my chest but then heard her sniffling. She asked, "Are you and Mommy ever getting back together?" and I had to say, "No, honey, we're not."

But the worst moment happened one evening when Cory, wise beyond his years, said to me, "Do you ever cry, Dad?" The question left me dumbstruck, because just about all I'd done for months was cry, at least when alone. I'd come to be surprised on any morning when my eyes looked mostly normal instead of red and puffy. But when Cory asked this question, I realized he hadn't seen me cry, not even once, perhaps, in all the time since his mom and I had split. No, there was one time, I realized. I'd been with the kids in the car, listening to music. In my car we listen to music all the time, because, well, I love music, and so do the kids. We have a wide range of artists on rotation constantly, representing all eras and genres, from Bruce Springsteen to ABBA, Count Basie to KISS.

On this day, Billy Joel was on: "Lullabye (Goodnight, My Angel)," which he wrote for his daughter, Alexa. It's a gorgeous heart-ripper of a song. You might find, as I did during my breakup, that your cry impulse is right near the surface all the time. Sometimes you can keep it at bay, while at other times you're helpless to do so. The song came on, I glimpsed Alisha in the back seat doing nothing but looking innocent and perfect, and I broke. Cory was in the back as well, Dustin up front with me. I tried to look out the window as my tears started to surge, but there was no way to stop them. *(Damn you, Billy. Not really, though. Love you, Billy.)* I felt bad for my kids because I didn't want them to have to deal with the weirdness of their big old dad weeping like a baby.

Trying to hide my emotions from them was the wrong decision — then, now, and at any time. When Cory asked me whether I ever cried, I understood that I must have at some point decided that, since my ex was crying a lot, it was up to me to be the strong one. I'd clenched my jaw and hidden my sadness and decided I would be their rock in the storm. But Cory obviously wasn't seeing me as strong; he was seeing me as unfeeling. Not only had I destroyed the world he'd known, but, far worse, I had been acting, in his eyes, indifferent toward having done so.

I also realized that my kids needed answers, explanations, any information they could use to make sense of why their world had been turned upside down, and I was giving them nothing. (I said I made a lot of mistakes, didn't I?) Although there are almost no good answers, one can at least be honest and real. I was being neither. Many moments during the kids' lives had made me realize they were smarter than I thought, were more mature than I imagined, and could handle more than I gave them credit for. Now I realized that while I thought I had been protecting them by not showing my feelings, I had in fact been lying. And I soon discovered that letting them into what I was feeling, even just a little, helped start to make things better.

Finally, when Cory asked if I ever cried, something else hit me hard. I suddenly remembered all of the conversations I'd had with other men about the pain. During the gut-wrenching period of my own split, I'd spoken to many guys — through work, at the gym, during support meetings, via other circles — some in the midst of a breakup themselves, some who were considering it, some who suspected it was coming, some who were trying to recover from one. Most of these men had described feelings of profound sadness and the inability to manage those feelings. One of them had said, "I feel like such a wimp. I cry about everything." Another had told me, "I feel like it's right there all the time, ready to burst. It takes nothing." A third had declared, not so delicately, "I feel like a hormonal woman. Everything makes me start sobbing. It's brutal." Another, starting to break down during our conversation, had said, through his sniffles, "Sorry, buddy — I guess I'm just a bit fucked up right now."

I understood what each of them meant, because I had been experiencing the same feelings. In high school, I wrote a short story called "Cuticle Tears." It was about a boy whose old-school father teaches him that real men don't cry. The kid suppresses his impulse to cry so much over time that, when the emotional dam inevitably breaks, other parts of his body start "crying" instead, meaning tears start to come through places other than his tear ducts, like his cuticles. I felt kind of like that boy those days: doing everything possible to keep my tears inside, in every context — at work, with my parents, in front of my kids — and my whole body threatening to rupture from the constant effort. All these other men were describing variations on this same theme. About my age, they were men of this apparently evolved generation, allegedly unafraid to show their emotions. These men were generally strong, fit, and confident, with comfortable lives, relative security, close families, and supportive friends. And they were all putting on a brave face, projecting strength when they were actually about to come apart.

That's when I thought about writing this book. I'd read a lot of books about marriage breakups, family transformation, and the effect of divorce on kids. (Real pick-me-ups, those books.) I thought about the fact that what helped me most during these nightmarish months was talking to other dads, hearing their stories, commiserating with them, and exchanging lots of hugs. I remembered each one of those conversations. The friend who told me he bottomed out when he found himself crying in the tool shed one night as an alternative to going back inside. The guy who said, "I started drinking. Then I realized I don't drink." The friend of a friend who told me, "This is shitty — like, colossally shitty. But there's shittier."

All these voices sounded like mine, expressing the same emotions and wanting the same thing: the trust, closeness, and affection of their kids, whom they cared about more than anything in the world. I decided to write this book for the many different men I've met and spoken to in the past few years, plus all those I haven't.

There's one guy in particular I wanted to write this book for, someone I spent only a few hours with: Vic, who I met in a support group. Big guy, teddy-bear type. We were in a small room in a community centre, just six of us, three guys and three women, plus the two counsellors leading the session. We were going around the room sharing stories. Everyone's was bad, of course. There was Yanelle, the newcomer from Cameroon whose husband had told her he was gay but wouldn't leave the marriage for fear of backlash from the African community. A man named Segundo, originally from Argentina, whose ex was trying to take him to the cleaners for what little money he had. The woman of East Indian heritage, Manisha, trying to hold down her supermarket job while also dealing with the enigma that is family court. Esteban, who had recently arrived to Canada from Spain, in a white T-shirt and leather jacket, moving a toothpick around his mouth while asking why the rules seemed to be so in favour of moms when he was the more involved parent.

When it was Vic's turn to speak, he talked about his three kids. He gestured with his hands a lot and stumbled with his words. His two younger kids, a son and daughter aged ten and twelve, seemed to be doing okay, adapting to the change, acting pretty cool with both parents. Then there was his sixteen-year-old daughter, who hadn't spoken to him in nearly a year. Vic was trying everything possible to get through to her: texting, writing her letters, connecting on social media, sending messages through her friends, trying to get clues from his two other kids about how he might crack through her anger. It didn't matter what he tried. She was behaving as though he didn't exist.

During the journey of researching and planning this book, I've encountered suffering in an unfortunately staggering variety. But I've never seen pain as helpless and bare as the pain I saw on Vic's face. At that moment I forgot all about my own grief. I wished I could do two things. The first was to give this huge tormented man a hug. The second was to let his daughter know he was dying inside, and that he would give up everything in life just to be able to feel her love again. This book is for Vic, and everyone else like him carrying that kind of pain.

It's bad, it's bad, it's bad, and then, one day, it's good. This book isn't meant to try to fool you into thinking things are going to be good tomorrow. It's meant to help you look inside yourself, understand and process your pain, cut yourself some slack, and hear from many other dads going through the same crap. They're all going to be okay, and so are you. So, if you're cool with it, I'd like to start by talking about you.

1

Managing Your Pain

We look before and after
And pine for what is not;
Our sincerest laughter
With some pain is fraught;
Our sweetest songs are those that tell of saddest thought.

— PERCY BYSSHE SHELLEY

When kids are involved, even the smoothest breakup brings a flood of sadness and an ocean of pain. It is big, crazy-ass, wow-I-didn't-know-this-kind-of-pain-existed pain, because it happens to involve the little people whom you love more than your own life. That thing that happens to others has now happened to you, and it sucks in a titanic way. Whereas in the past you've been all *Roll with the punches* and *Let's attack this problem* and *I can play through the pain*, this maelstrom is making you want to just curl up in a corner. You probably feel confused and burdened. Maybe you feel, privately, a little sorry for yourself. Odds are you also feel angry at yourself for feeling this self-pity.

You may have experienced emotional pain before that you could ignore, escape, or redirect. In my case, there was nothing I had felt that couldn't be cured by a hockey game with the guys, which always left me feeling happily drained and exhilarated, or a few hours of focused writing, which made me feel energized and industrious. However, marital breakup brings a quality of pain that is total and relentless. Maybe you've always been the kind of guy who got out of bed smiling at what the day might bring, and now you feel bummed out more or less around the clock. Maybe the scope of things that make you smile has narrowed down to your kids and not much else, and you're wondering if that's ever going to change.

A recent movie, *Unbroken,* was about Louie Zamperini, an Olympic runner turned World War II bombardier who, after surviving a plane crash and nearly two months adrift on the Pacific, was found by a Japanese patrol boat and imprisoned in POW camps. In one scene, the sadistic Japanese officer of the camp makes Louie hold a concrete slab over his head and orders the guard to shoot the prisoner if he drops it. Louie stands in agony, holding the slab above his head as the hot sun beats down. But he keeps it there. The other prisoners look on in horror as the hours pass. Eventually relief comes to Louie — I won't tell you how — and one day relief will come to you too. Right now you might feel like you're holding that slab over your head all day. But, believe me, it's going to get lighter.

The pain of my family split was a massive shock to the system because I had led, for forty years, a fairly crisis-free life. The confusion and complexity of the breakup swamped me emotionally, psychologically, and spiritually. At such times, our self-talk can be brutal. Here's a small sampling of the things I found I was saying to myself at different stages:

- I did something at some point and this is my punishment. Okay, I don't believe in existential payback like that because it seems way too simple, but too bad, that's what I'm going with. This is penance. Or something.
- What do I know about anything? How can I be part of a decision that affects five people when I'm only one person? How can I be part of giving three children life and then

> pull the rug out from under those lives? What did they
> do to deserve this? Nothing, you jerk. Man, I can't believe
> what a selfish jerk you are.
- Could somebody up there please give me the answer to make this better? *Please?*
- Man, I wish I were religious. I bet that would make this so much easier. (Or maybe not. You can read about my visit to the rabbi in Chapter 11.)

Needless to say, none of this self-talk was helpful, because of how, as you know, life doesn't solve stuff for you and you have to eventually deal with it. But for months the pain came in waves, constantly threatening to pull me under. I knew they were coming, but knowing did not make them any less powerful. I felt like I was getting caught in the undertow, tossed around, battered against the rocks, and spat out onto the beach, only to wait for the next set of waves. Even worse was the fact that the waves were impossible to predict. There was no signal; they'd just rise up and wash over me. Even at times when I thought I was having a decent day or doing an okay job of keeping myself together, something would happen to bring on another tsunami.

The worst of these moments occurred when I was in the car driving to work one morning, feeling good from an early swim. I was listening to a sports radio program in which a pair of tickets was being offered for that night's hockey game to the caller who gave the best reason to have them. The first two calls were typical: a guy who'd been a long-time fan but had never been to a game; another who wanted to surprise a buddy for his birthday. And then a young girl's voice came on the line. Logically, I should have switched off the radio then and there. But, you know, we *Homo sapiens*, we love to see how much pain we can stand. This sweet little thing explained to the hosts that her parents had divorced the previous year, and the courts had decided she could see her dad only every other weekend, and she loved him a lot and missed him every day, so it would be nice to do something special with him.

As I write this today, nearly five years later, I am barely able to type the story without breaking down, so you can pretty much guess my state while hearing the call back then. I pulled over and sobbed for, I don't know, a while. On days like that, when the pain was so immense, I would often think, *How is this not killing me?* I felt by turns numb, raw, empty, hopeless, helpless ... just kind of woozy with anguish, perhaps the emotional analog of when you experience such a physical pain that you nearly black out, but not quite.

Speaking of which, did you ever see the movie *Dances with Wolves*? It's a favourite of mine. I particularly like the opening scene: Kevin Costner's character, a disillusioned Civil War lieutenant named John Dunbar, in a medical tent listening to the doctors discuss whether to amputate his ravaged foot, decides he's having none of it. Sweating and nearly breathless from the pain, he forces himself to put his boot back on over his blood-soaked foot; and as he does so, nearly passing out, a sound comes out of him that is almost like laughter. The reason I like this moment so much is because I feel Costner as an actor really nails it — he is marvelling at the degree of pain he is in while still somehow enduring it. That is a bit like how I felt every day during the first months after my breakup. I would wager it's close to how you feel too.

On many days I assumed I would eventually have a heart attack from the stress. I was in pretty good shape, but I still half-expected a shooting pain up my left arm at some point. Didn't happen, thankfully. The pain of those days also made me think a lot about when my kids were babies and my ex and I were, like any new parents, so exhausted we could have been mistaken for zombies, but managed to somehow endure it, as all parents do. I remember having the revelation at the time that the only reason parents survive this level of sleep deprivation is that they know, or maybe their bodies do, that if they don't keep functioning, their kids will be the worse for it.

The pain of a family breakup is similar, substituting your body in the first situation for your heart in the second. You know that, no matter how great your pain, if you don't stay present and able, your kids will suffer. And, as every parent knows, there's nothing you wouldn't do to prevent your kids from suffering. Because of this, you're more resilient and adaptable than you think. You have the ability to persevere even when the grief feels so heavy it might suffocate you.

On the worst of those days, when my heart felt so dark and the outlook so bleak, the reassuring thing, if there was one, was that I was surviving it. This was a level of pain that was astonishing in its force and persistence, yet I was living to tell the tale. I'd wake up every morning feeling two things in parallel: (1) *I can't believe how much this hurts*; and (2) *I can't believe I'm waking up to experience it again*. (For suggestions on keeping yourself safe when feeling desperate or overwhelmed, see Chapter 6. If you feel you're in crisis and unable to manage your emotions or behaviours, please seek professional help right away.)

Sometimes, absorbing the simple wisdom of others helped calm me down or lift me up in dark moments. The famous Nigerian poet and novelist Ben Okri wrote, "The most authentic thing about us is our capacity to create, to overcome, to endure, to transform, to love, and to be greater than our suffering." Think about every part of that quote. We create, meaning we make something out of every day, because that's why we're here. We overcome, meaning we don't cruise through life; we face obstacles and determine how to get past them. We endure, meaning life throws different things at us and we absorb them and move ever forward. We transform, meaning there is no moment in which we do not change, no day in which we do not grow. We love, meaning the care we feel for others can help us rise above our own individual circumstances. And we are greater than our suffering, meaning pain, along with joy, is part of the human condition, but we survive, and we persist.

The U2 song "Stuck in a Moment You Can't Get Out Of" also offers some wisdom. Bono wrote the song about the suicide of Michael Hutchence, his close friend and the lead singer of INXS. He said that he wrote it in the form of an argument in which he tries to convince his friend of the foolishness of such an act. So the song is depicting a fight he felt guilty about never having had. "It's a row between mates," Bono said. "You're kinda trying to wake them up out of an idea. I feel the biggest respect I could pay to him was not to write some stupid soppy song, so I wrote a really tough, nasty little number." I like Bono's message about the impetus for the song: his wanting to budge his friend out of a mental state that was dragging him into darkness.

When you experience a breakup as a dad, you are in the midst of the most painful transition of your life. At moments the pain seems nearly impossible to withstand. But I am here to tell you that, with time, you will get through. (I am also here to tell you that I know how annoying it is when people say things like "You will get through this," and that the normal reaction to people telling you this is to want to drill them in the solar plexus. So I understand if you want to do that to me right now, even if what I'm saying is true.)

As for this irritating "time" thing ... we might as well talk about it, since you're going to hear about it repeatedly from friends, professionals, family members, and, especially, others who have gone through a family breakup (like me). I didn't mind maybe the first instance in which someone told me that time was necessary for the pain to heal, and my kids to make the transition, and my ex and me to find a new normal, *et cetera*, *ad nauseam*, *ad infinitum*. I nodded politely, because I knew the person telling me this was just trying to help, even though my private internal reply was, *That's awesome, thanks. You've just made things even worse by telling me there's nothing I can do except endure this emotional torture and wait to see if things get better over an indeterminate period.*

Then the next person said it, then another. "Just needs time, I.J. Time heals all wounds. Time will do its work. Kids mature, exes settle down, and hurt subsides." Boy, did I find this annoying. It was like walking through hell and having to stop at regular checkpoints to have people say, "Keep walking. That's all the information you get. Ha ha ha ha!"

The thing is, all those people trying to give you some hope to latch onto are right, at least mostly. Think of it like a spectrum, where the moment of your telling your kids the awful news is the far left — that is, the worst — side, and the proverbial light at the end of the tunnel the far right. That side is yet to be defined, since you don't know what is going to eventually represent a state of "better," or "healed," or "whole," or "I no longer feel like I want to commit *hara-kiri* on a daily basis."

Unfortunately, there is no other starting point on this journey than the extreme left side of the spectrum. No family breakup starts in the middle. Even in splits where the kids, on some level, know it's better, this is still the lousiest news they're ever going to hear. But, just as what goes up must come down, when you start at the extreme left side of anything, the only direction you can go is right (pun intended). None of you as individuals, you as a family, will stagnate in one spot, because we don't exist in a state of inertia; we change and adapt. Progression through the spectrum won't be steady or linear, but it starts the day after the worst day, when you and your family are launched by a metaphorical slingshot from a normal, happy existence all the way to the far left side.

When your family breaks up, every part of the daily existence you've known becomes practically splintered and emotionally fractured. That day is equivalent to one end of the spectrum — the most depressing day, when darkness reigns. But it's also the day that starts everything moving in the other direction. When things feel their darkest, light must inevitably re-emerge. You, and your kids, will travel from the one end of the spectrum to the other. The transition will take time, and it will take some work. But you'll get through it. Together.

Painful Gifts

My son Cory loves rock 'n' roll and is a huge Bruce Springsteen fan. He dressed like "The Boss" one Halloween, with a little guitar and a red bandana sticking out the back pocket of his jeans. He spent a whole summer listening to "Born to Run" and "Thunder Road" pretty much exclusively. We've spent countless hours discussing Wendy in the former and Mary in the latter.

When Springsteen finally wrote an autobiography and the publication date was announced as a week before Cory's birthday, I was stoked. Bruce had penned the thing himself, which I knew would make it much better than a ghostwritten bio. Plus, Cory was extremely angry at me about the split, and I thought this might be a way to bridge the gap.

I bought the book the day it came out. On the morning of Cory's birthday, I watched him open it. He put it aside without saying anything and proceeded to open the other gifts. As soon as I left the house that day, he asked my ex to return the book. Never read a page. So that really sucked. A few months later, at Hanukkah, the only way I was able to get a gift to Cory was to buy it for him and then ask Alisha to pretend it was from her. That sucked too.

Pain of any kind is tiring. When you have a virus, you feel drained because your body is waging an internal war. You may have had physical pain before — a bad ankle sprain, a dislocated shoulder, a torn ligament — and you know that the rehabilitation from such injuries can be gruelling. Even small ailments, like cankers, blisters, or headaches, demand energy from your body to fight and heal. That said, the emotional pain of a split is more draining than any injury you've ever had. Combine the hurt with having constant arguments between you and your ex, and trying to help your kids through their own grief, and you're working with an engine running constantly on empty.

I call this sensation pain-fatigue: the raw pain itself plus the fatigue that ensues from it. This pain-fatigue can really take the spit and vinegar out of you. And just as we sometimes feel like we'd do anything for really bad physical pain to go away, at times you start to think it might be better for your kids if you withdrew from the interminable fighting, allowing them peace instead of being caught in the middle of constant rancour.

That's the pain-fatigue talking. Shake those thoughts away. Don't ever give up — on yourself or on your kids — even though at times, bizarrely, surrendering might seem like the thing to do because you're just so worn down. As my friend Marcello puts it, "As hard as it gets, and as sensible as it might seem to throw up your hands and just say, 'I quit,' to make your life easier, don't."

Lindsey Jay Walsh, a marriage and family therapist with Pear Tree Family Therapy in Winnipeg, says, "Believe it or not, the most common mistake I see dads make with their kids is giving up. I honestly think there are a lot fewer 'deadbeat' dads than our society would lead us to believe. However, I do think that there are a lot of 'I don't know what to do now' dads who feel so disparaged and defeated that they give up hope."

The pain-fatigue is one thing that may get you down. The no-filter innocence of kids is another. After the family breakup, one home is going to become two, and, in most cases, it's the dad who will create the new one. During this process, your kids may say and do lots of things that feel like gut-punches to you, like making unfavourable comparisons between your home and Mom's home, or resisting being at the "new" place at all. Know that they are not saying such things to hurt you. They just don't like change, and, of course, they censor nothing. Noted family counsellor and author of *Honey, I Wrecked the Kids* Alyson Schafer says:

Dads can take their kids' comments and behaviors personally, to the point where it makes them feel like going away. Any kid is going to moan and groan about having to change and adjust, but while they're really just saying, "I like my own bed and stuffed animals," it can be easy to hear this as, "They don't love me as much." This can grind fathers down to the point where they're ready to say, "Fine, stay at Mom's." They take it more as a personal directive than a developmentally appropriate way of kids bemoaning the situation.

It's not that you'd ever make a knowing decision to see less of your kids. But the pain-fatigue can warp your thinking, and so can the wrong interpretation of, as Schafer puts it, "developmentally appropriate" aversion to change. A number of men told me something along the lines of "I convinced myself that the right thing to do for my kids would be to back off, because I didn't want them to be in the middle of a war all the time."

Of course, *any* choice is better than backing away. These guys at some point convinced themselves that not fighting for their kids was the noble thing to do — and then they all eventually snapped out of it. The thing your kids need most is to know how much you love them, how you are devoted to them, and how you will always be there for them. On that note, let's talk more about your kids.

Words to Remember

Here are ten sayings that are similar to "What doesn't kill you makes you stronger," to remind you that you're going to get through this crapstorm.

> "Sometime the only way t' keep goin' is t' keep goin'."
> — BODIE THOENE

"Don't pray for lighter burdens, but for stronger backs."

— BUDDHA

"Heroism is endurance for one moment more."

— GEORGE F. KENNAN

"Even the darkest night will end and the sun will rise."

— VICTOR HUGO

"Sometimes there's not a better way. Sometimes there's only the hard way."

— MARY E. PEARSON

"We are healed from suffering only by experiencing it to the full."

— MARCEL PROUST

"The bamboo that bends is stronger than the oak that resists."

— JAPANESE PROVERB

"Some days there won't be a song in your heart. Sing anyway."

— EMORY AUSTIN

"The world breaks everyone and afterward many are strong at the broken places."

— ERNEST HEMINGWAY

And my favourite:

"If you're going through hell, keep going."

— ATTRIBUTED TO WINSTON CHURCHILL

2

Guiding Your Kids

Kids like knowing what to expect. They crave routine and stability, and they resist change. That's why parenting books urge you to establish a nighttime routine, to be consistent with consequences, and to stay patient when your toddler wants to sing the same bedtime song forty-seven nights in a row. Even for adults, change is hard; for kids, it's a real beast. And when change happens to the one thing that anchors their life the most — their family — it's like dropping a bomb into a quiet pond. Helping your children through this adjustment is extremely difficult and complicated. Nothing you do feels right; everything you say seems wrong. How are you supposed to explain to your children that you and your partner have agreed to shatter their lives? They need to know the breakup wasn't their fault, so you tell them it wasn't. But if it wasn't their fault, then it was your fault, or her fault, or the fault of you both. You don't want to assign blame, but you also don't want to say nothing was wrong.

They want to know if this change means everything else is changing too. Trying to talk to them about the change feels like you are digging a hole deeper and deeper, and watching them helplessly fall. They keep giving you chances to explain the situation, and, no matter how much you prepare your answers or how many articles you read, you keep confusing them more. Truth said, there are no easy or quick answers. Kids need to go through the stages of loss and grief just as adults do. Less important than giving the right answers is simply showing them you're there, just as you have always been.

In the wake of this tempest, it's critical that you do all you can to ensure that your kids continue to feel anchored. The familiar is pleasant and reassuring; the unfamiliar can be frightening as hell. Your kids have been forced to leave behind their normal existence and instead have been dropped into a dark, gaping hole of uncertainty. You may understand in your grown-up mind all the reasons why this change will be better for all of you, but they don't have the experience or perspective to grasp that same understanding. Imagine the change for them is like an earthquake. One minute you're standing on the same solid earth you've always stood on, and then, without warning, it cracks and splits, and you feel like you might be swallowed up. That's how your breakup feels for your kids. The dependable bedrock of family they've relied on has suddenly fractured, and, for all they know, that fissure is just going to keep getting wider.

Every earthquake is different, just as every family split is its own seismic event. The goal for you and your ex is to manage the aftershocks and help your kids understand that the ground underfoot will reconstitute slowly, over time, and again become solid, if changed.

So what are you supposed to do to help your kids feel tethered during a period of such turmoil? How can you give them assurance that life will go on, and allow them to feel continuity amid chaos? Published family counsellor Alyson Schafer has a great metaphor for this. She describes a kid's world as being like a snow globe, an environment in which everything is pleasantly self-contained. A family breakup is like a violent shaking of that snow globe. Helping them cope with that unexpected tumult means showing them that everything within the world of their snow globe is still there, and that the flakes just need time to settle. "You need to reassure your kids that everything in there is still the same," Schafer says. "Friends. School. Pets. Programs. When it all lands, it's just going to be in a different arrangement."

What does this mean in practice? What do you tell them, and show them, to reassure them that everything in the snow globe is still there? There are two components to this. First, the practical; second, the emotional. The practical bits are the things that form the tangible fabric of kids' daily lives: going to school, seeing friends, watching movies, playing sports. The more they can see evidence that these things still exist, the faster they can accept the change.

Let's break these practical elements into three categories: daily stuff, non-daily-but-regular stuff, and spontaneous stuff. Daily stuff includes all the activities that act as the collective glue of your kids' existence: things like you helping them do their homework in the evening and packing their school lunches in the morning. It includes rituals like dinner, bath, and bedtime, and intangible threads like inside family jokes, or songs you've made up together.

Non-daily-but-regular stuff likewise consists of activities that give your kids a feeling of relative normalcy via the recognition that there are things to count on and look forward to, at predictable times and intervals — piano lesson on Saturday morning, band practice after school on Wednesday, track practice before school on Thursday, dinner at the grandparents' on Friday. Amid such upheaval, these regular events help remind them that the good things are not disappearing.

Third, the spontaneous stuff includes all those fun things you do that they need to know you'll continue to do. It would be bad enough for them to think that the dependable parts of their schedule are going away. It would be *really* bad for them to think that the unexpected, fun stuff is going away too, because that's a big part of what makes you Dad. For me, that means tossing them in the air, playing Pillow Whap (a game in which I swing a pillow back and forth while they jump up and down on the bed trying to avoid it — it's so fun), suplexing them into bed at night, going on hikes, exploring caves, having Just Dance competitions, swimming in the rain, and lying down on the grass to watch the clouds. Do everything you can to show your kids that all three of these practical areas of their life still exist.

When you first detonate the shell of the family split, it seems to your kids like their world is ending, because the one part they thought would never change is changing. Because of this, it seems that all bets are off on every other part of their lives too. You can immediately start to bring them back from that shock by showing them that the different components of their lives are still intact, from the things that occur like clockwork to the stuff you do on the spur of the moment. The first thing my ex and I did with our kids after announcing our split to them was to watch a movie together in the family room. We were trying to send the message that, even though the two of us were breaking up, we as their parents weren't going anywhere.

That's the practical stuff. Equally important for you to monitor and nurture is the emotional side of your children's lives. I believe there are three parts to this as well: communicating clearly and honestly, even if the truth hurts; acting positively toward your spouse during the breakup; and being consistently present for your kids.

First, communication. This topic could take up a book on its own, as could the mistakes I made in communicating, or not communicating, with my kids to help them through the family breakup. One piece of advice from all the experts I spoke to was to ask your children how they're feeling. I'm embarrassed to say that I mistakenly decided it was my job to protect my kids from their own feelings. This was just a bad decision made with good intentions. Part of your parenting job, not just in the midst of family breakup but regarding anything in your kids' lives, is to help them acknowledge, process, and deal with their feelings, not build a shield against them.

I wish I had been aware of Schafer's great metaphor then. "Give a lot of affection and caring," she counsels, "so that the snow globe settles as fast as possible. Your kids might be thinking, for example, 'I'm never going to see my cousins on Dad's side again.' If you don't create the opportunities for them to express those kinds of feelings, you can't address them."

Even more surprising to me than the advice about sharing feelings was the suggestion of most experts to involve the kids in the separation process. Not the legal process, but the emotional and practical one. I, like many parents, wanted to keep such details hidden from my kids, believing this would help them cope better. I would often say things like, "You guys don't need to worry about that. Your only job is to be kids." I realize now that telling them this probably only made them feel as if they weren't part of a decision or a process that had upended their world, increasing the sense of helplessness they probably already felt.

"Though it may not feel intuitive to do so, involve your children in the process of change," says Toronto psychotherapist Kyle Karalash. "Solicit their opinions and thoughts. The stress of change has the greatest impact when it is slapped down in front of us without warning, and without apparent consideration of how we're feeling. Parents often make the mistake of keeping children on the outside because they want to protect them, when in fact this only creates more anxiety. Being involved in the process can help them deal with it."

When they do ask questions, keep the answers simple. Me, I tend to overtalk. My kids like to tease me about it. Numerous times I've stopped a lecture or explanation in its second or third minute to ask, "When did you tune out?" and they replied, "A while ago." Many times they would ask me a question about the split, and I would give them an unsatisfactory answer. They would reply with silence, causing me to bungle my way through some equally useless explanation, in response to which their befuddled silence would continue, and so on. This was not a demonstration of effective post-split communication.

I've since learned that simple works better than complicated. "One of the most important things you can do to try to break down your kids' confusion is to explain things in simple ways" says Karalash. "The most difficult part for them is their confusion about what's going to happen, what this will mean to their lives. They can't prepare for something they don't understand. Help them." Keep it simple, but do communicate constantly with your kids during this period of internal havoc. Their biggest fear is the unknown, including whether they are going to lose you.

Recently, I heard from my daughter, Alisha, "When you told us that you and Mommy were breaking up, I didn't know if I was ever going to see you again." I was floored when she said this. I thought I was going to cry forever. I was definitely going to hate myself forever. That aside, her comment highlighted something important to me: I had seen that moment through my own lens, which was the lens that said, *We're breaking up as your parents, but we're still your mom and dad, and we will always love you, provide for you, protect you, and support you. I will still tuck you in at night, and read you stories, and tell you jokes, and teach you things, and coach you in sports, and wipe your tears.*

But that was what *I* knew. Alisha didn't know any of that. All she'd heard was the first part: Mommy and Daddy are breaking up. After she told me that, every night at bedtime I would tell her to put up her index finger, and I'd do the same. "How many daddies do you have?" I'd ask her. "One," she'd say. "And how many daughters do I have?" I'd ask her. "One," she'd say. Then we'd touch index fingers, I'd kiss her forehead, and I'd tuck her in.

The danger of doing what I did at first — communicating less instead of more — is that your children, who are already confused and scared, may retreat further into themselves instead of opening up, and this in turn may hinder, instead of smooth, the path to healing. "In my experience," says Karalash, "the time taken to adjust to the new family dynamics and routines depends deeply on how actively and openly the parents communicate with their children. If the children sense secrets and tension, they'll behave accordingly. Often parents fear asking, but your children have a voice and they want to use it. Check in, see where they're at. Saying things as simple as 'I know there have been a lot of changes lately. How you are doing?' can help a lot."

One caveat here: there is a difference between giving your kids a voice and unintentionally asking them to make decisions that ought to be the responsibility of you and your ex. This point came home to me recently when I asked Alisha if she'd like me or Mommy to take her to her swimming lesson, which occurred on the cusp of one of our transfer periods. I said this because I wanted to seem generous and flexible. I thought, in fact, that I was being rather cool about it and gave myself a mental pat on the back. But Alisha replied, "Daddy, it makes me uncomfortable when you do that. I don't want to have to choose." Her response was an eye-opening moment.

Winnipeg therapist Lindsey Jay Walsh describes this behaviour as inadvertently giving children the wrong kind of power, which is unfair. "Kids really struggle when they don't feel that the world is a safe place," he says. "The fracture between their parents can degrade their sense that

Mom and Dad are strong enough to help them make sense of the world, which is the first and most important ongoing role that they play. After the split, if the two of you can't communicate well, it can put the kids in the very stressful and uncomfortable position of feeling they have way too much power over family events."

Your kids can also experience stress if they feel they can influence you or your ex to pre-empt decisions made by the other. Here's a simple guideline. If a decision involves stuff the kids are doing just with you, involve them as much or as little as you see fit. If, on the other hand, a decision involves stuff with your ex, that's up to your ex, and you should stay out of it. And if a decision involves stuff that the two of you need to manage, talk about it first before you involve the kids, so they see that you still organize things together, they know you're both still involved in making important decisions, and the two of you can be consistent.

Birthdays are a good example of items that need co-management. If you and your ex discuss ideas first, you can then say to your son or daughter, "Mommy and I were talking about what to do for your birthday. Three ideas we thought you might like are this, this, and that. What do you think?" If you skip the preliminary step of conversing with your ex, a negative conversational chain can easily take root, in which your kid goes back to Mommy and reports that you talked about birthday ideas. Then you get a call from your ex asking why you spoke to the child about it before she did, and so on. As I said, use simple guidelines here. For stuff both you and your ex are going to be involved in, talk about it first, then get the kids' input, if warranted. If a decision falls within the context of you and the kids alone, on your time, open up that roundtable and have a blast. If it's on your ex's time, butt out.

Similarly, avoid making judgments about anything your ex does, and don't let the kids bait you into giving them ammunition to take back to her, such as when you get a call from your son, with the phone strategically on speaker, and he poses a question like "Mommy won't let me stay up to watch the basketball game tonight because she says I'll be tired for school tomorrow. Daddy, do you think that's fair?" Again, establish and enforce the rules in your environment, but don't fall into the trap of giving your views on what should be happening on the other side. Be clear with the kids that you will not give opinions on how your ex-partner or on the rules she enforces. The only proper answer to the question above is "Those are Mommy's rules, honey. If you feel they're unfair, talk to her about them."

Part of communication is letting your kids know, repeatedly and in different ways, that the breakup had nothing to do with them. This statement probably feels simple to you, but for them, it requires repetition and reinforcement. A lot of it. "They need assurance that they aren't the cause, and that they will still receive the same love and support from both of their parents," says Karalash. "They may feel worried that their parents splitting means they won't receive the same care and support, or that they're unloved, or that they'll be rejected." Make this part simple for them, and repeat it often. Your breakup wasn't their fault. As frustrating an answer as it is for them, the only true one is that adult relationships are complicated and sometimes they end, even when you didn't think they would.

Another important part of communication with your kids is being consistent with the message that the split has happened, is real, and is not going to change. Saying this will hurt every time, but it's the only proper message to give to your kids. Offering false hope unfairly hampers their ability to accept, and thus work through, the change. There will likely be plenty of moments in which you'll be tempted to dilute or even change the message. I remember so many awful exchanges in which one of the kids would say to me something like "Why do you hate Mommy?" and I'd say, "I don't hate Mommy," and they'd say, "Then why don't you want to be her husband?" and so on. Or they would ask me if we were going to get back together and I would want to give them a reply such as "I don't know. We're going through a hard time right now," just to avoid the guilt of shooting one more dagger into their little hearts. Or my ex and I would be standing at the front door of the house together getting ready to take the kids somewhere, and one of them would insist I hug my ex, or tell her she looked pretty, or name her three best qualities.

These were excruciatingly difficult moments. Watching the desperation on my kids' faces was searing. Unfortunately, sometimes the only way to help someone through something is to give them the bad news in an unadulterated way. You can't move on from something until you accept that it's happened. So when your kids ask if you're getting back together with your ex, the best answer you can give them is no. Even while you're giving them that cruel answer, you're also holding them in your arms, and that's what will let them know that they can handle this information.

The second part of keeping your kids emotionally anchored is acting positive and supportive toward your ex within the context of the breakup. If your children see you demonstrating a healthy dynamic toward your ex, this will help to reduce their anxiety and allow them to understand that they, too, can get to a positive place. It will let them focus not on the bad blood between the two of you, but rather on your efforts to get along. It will show them they still have a mommy and daddy who love them unconditionally, and will prevent them from feeling that they're in the middle of a tug-of-war.

According to Dipti Shah, a family and systemic psychotherapist and integrative counsellor at the London Child and Family Therapy Centre in the United Kingdom:

> One of the biggest dilemmas parents get caught up in during a breakup is trying to win their kids' loyalty by overtly or covertly bad-mouthing the other parent. The most difficult part for kids is having to manage what they may see as this division. They already face the task of having to see the parents as separate and start living under two roofs. The internal process of managing this change can be emotionally and psychologically overwhelming, without the additional trauma of Mom and Dad trying to get them on their side. The split is about you, not the children. Though the split may be a good thing, it is not their choice, and finding a way of overcoming personal differences when co-parenting can minimize the challenges for them and even help them become more resilient later.

Even when you think you're being subtle or private with your comments or gestures, you're probably not. Toronto-based psychologist

Andrew Shaul notes that one of the biggest mistakes he sees split dads making is what he calls letting anger leak. "Rolling eyes, making faces, those kinds of behaviours," he says. "You may think these things aren't noticeable, but they are. *All* of them. However warranted your feelings may be, don't put them onto your kids. They had nothing to do with this. And feeling like they have to choose who's right and who's wrong tears them apart."

You will experience moments, maybe frequent ones, in which you feel lots of nasty stuff bubbling up and you really want to let it out, by saying something directly to your ex in front of the kids or via comments about your ex. Don't. It isn't worth it. "Whatever anger you have, however justified," says Shaul, "don't get into the little editorial comments. All that does is give your kids the sense that, to be close to you, they have to dislike their mom. It's not going to help. It is going to make them feel more confused and conflicted." The psychotherapist Karalash reinforces this point: "Parents separating is a lot for children to process. It can lead to feeling pressure to choose a side or constantly stand up for whichever parent they hear being targeted. Making them witness to arguments between you only forms a hostile environment for their growth."

Even worse than showing anger toward your ex is exposing your kids to arguments between the two of you about custody and schedules, which will create a level of anxiety they are not equipped to deal with. "Overhearing their parents argue over custody rights and visitations is devastating for kids," says Karalash. "The first thought they have hearing those discussions is, 'Will I still get to see my dad?' or 'If I live with Dad, do I see Mom less?'" Keep them miles away from that stuff. It's hard enough on you. Imagine what it does to them.

The third element of helping your kids through the emotional part of this transition is also the simplest, and one you'll see referred to again and again throughout these chapters: just be there. Their souls are going through mayhem. Nothing you do for them during this time is more important than merely being around. "Be accessible and present in a consistent manner," says Vancouver-based psychologist Dr. Rotem Regev.

Be available. Put. That. Phone. Away. You will miss so many cues for connecting with your kids. Let them know you're available, and be really present, attentive, and engaged. Playing cards on the carpet counts so much more than taking them to the movies. Consistency and predictability are the building blocks for a child's well-being. It creates their sense of trust in you, themselves, and the world.

Andrew Shaul echoes this view, saying that the best thing you can do for your kids to give them reassurance after the world-shaking news of Mommy and Daddy splitting up is "simply spending time with them. Words are nice, but actions speak louder. They need to know that, though you're leaving Mom, you're not leaving them."

From the first moment of your children's lives, you as parents are their rocks. You are who they trust, the people who give them security and direction. And while the things they may need from you at different stages may change, this basic principle does not. Your presence is the first thing your kids know in life, and it will never cease to be the most important. Presence means two things. First, being there when you're physically there, and second, being there when you're physically not. We're fortunate that there are so many ways to communicate today, so even on the days you aren't with your kids, you can still do many different things to ensure they feel your presence. You can't communicate or demonstrate that presence too much.

Spending time with your kids does not mean spoiling them, or trying to overcompensate for their pain through material offerings. Small expressions of caring and gestures of love, and even the ongoing presence of rules and routines, are far more important, and will help them stay connected to the life they're familiar with. "I sometimes hear dads doing the following math," says Dr. Regev. "'Something happened that made the kids sad, therefore I must do something that makes them happy.' Of course I admire you for wanting to make your kids happy. Holding their sadness tenderly will do that. Showering them with gifts, letting them watch more TV, and disrespecting boundaries will not."

In an episode of *The Simpsons* called "Lisa's Pony," Homer, as a response to his guilt over failing to replace daughter Lisa's saxophone reed, buys her a pony. The gift assuages his guilt for a while, until Homer realizes the one thing his daughter wants is for him to be interested in her life. That's what your kids want too: for you to get excited about what excites them, to be proud of them, to believe in them, to give them rules, and to forgive them when they spill stuff on the couch. You and your ex are the people who have defined your kids' boundaries every day of their lives. Don't stop doing this because you think loosening the reins is going to help them feel better right now. A lack of boundaries or rules will only make them feel less anchored to the familiar. Be present in all the ways your children want you, and need you, to be.

Despite all of your efforts, you may see your kids regressing in their behaviour or development. That's okay. It's a natural response to a cataclysmic event. As Alyson Schafer says, "They will likely be very clingy during this time. They're worried about security and attachment. They might ask for more baby-like treatment, like wanting to come into your bed at night. Give them that. Right now they need lots of proof that you're there and present, and that there's still lots of love."

Your kids' transition through family breakup is, to say the least, complicated. But by paying close attention to the elements of their practical and emotional lives and continually showing them that, even amid change, the most important things stay the same, you can help row them through the storm.

––––––––––––

Kids need their dads. It's interesting to me that the body of research showing why is relatively new. Intuitively, you know your kids benefit from your love and presence, but formal study on this topic has been relatively scant until recently, which tells you just how long traditional thinking about parental roles has held sway. There's a ton of literature on why kids need their moms. When it comes to dads, it isn't so much that there's been a negative bias; the lack of research is more like indifference.

Dads may feel this perception reinforced when their kids seem to gravitate more toward Mom in the midst of a breakup. My friend Marshall describes it like this:

> Early in the process, you might feel a bit left out, or that the love is flowing in only one direction. Most of the time, even if you are the perfect family, it just seems that kids naturally lean towards their mothers. When you separate, this imbalance seems to intensify. But children will come around. They realize how solid their life is with a good father who always makes time for them. It's my belief that fathers teach their children three things: how to respect, how to love, and how to be loved. Three simple but very important elements in life.

Never doubt the importance of your presence in your kids' lives. They may act out, they may tell you they hate you, they may describe their hope for your demise in lots of colourful and imaginative ways. They're kids; they're expressing their pain in the ways they know how. Don't go anywhere.

Why do kids need their dads? Oh, about a hundred reasons. Did you know that kids who have stable and involved dads fare better on nearly every cognitive, social, and emotional measure researchers have thought to devise? Did you know that kids whose dads are more involved in their lives are observed to be more sociable, more confident, more curious, more self-directed, more resilient in dealing with stress, better able to handle unusual situations, and less likely to act out in school or engage in risky behaviours when they're teens? That they're less likely to break the law, drop out of school, or engage in risky sex? That a father's presence is observed to have a positive influence on sibling and peer relationships, behaviour, achievement, and self-esteem? That kids with more involved dads suffer from fewer psychological problems and are less prone to obesity?

I could go on. This list isn't meant to be a rally for dads, or a contest with moms. It's meant to remind you that it isn't just nice for your kids when you're around; it makes a serious difference to their lives, no matter your demographic, ethnicity, or background. Across family structures, cultures, and circumstances, when fathers are engaged with their children, those children derive benefits that help them over the course of their lives.

Your relationship with your kids' mom may have run its course, but your relationship with your kids is forever. And if anyone tells you one parenting role is more important than the other, feel free to cite some or all of the above, or just do a quick online search for "why kids need their dads" and read any of the dozens of articles that come up. One school of thought even proposes that a father's love for his children is the most vital key to their development. Sigmund Freud himself said, "I cannot think of any need in childhood as strong as the need for a father's protection."

It pleases me that literature into dads' involvement and influence has emerged. Fathers today are pouring love and care into their relationships with their children, and it's good to see this acknowledged. According to one paper, fathers were spending a little under three hours per week on child care in 1965. By the turn of the twenty-first century, that figure had more than doubled. Most dads I know spend twice again that amount today.

––––––––

Despite the various ways your kids may naturally act out in response to this shock in their lives, they trust you to be their compass, their protector, and their constant source of love and reassurance. Try as much as possible to see and feel things through their lens, and you'll do well at helping them through the family transition. The first and most important thing to remember in any split, says Yshai Boussi, a licensed professional counsellor and family therapist specializing in adolescent and family therapy with Portland Family Counseling in Oregon, is "to focus first and foremost on the kids' needs. Remember that they didn't ask for this to happen and had no input or control over it." The biggest gift you can give them is understanding. Perhaps they will even, in time, come to see the event less as a tragedy than as a transformation. Perhaps time and maturity will allow them to adopt the perspective of the child who said, "I hate the term *broken family*. When my parents divorced, they didn't break the family, they fixed it. Their marriage was what was broken."

Professional golfer Adam Scott has an even more positive take. "The divorce in my family was really amicable," he says. "There were no fireworks. It was all sort of behind the scenes, if you will. None of us kids ever saw any argument." Now, I don't want to be all Pollyanna about this. A surplus of quotes talk about how hard divorce is on kids and how it continues to affect them throughout their lives. But remember that there are an equal number of quotes like the ones above, which show that if parents behave well and things are handled with relative peace and optimism, kids can not only get through the divorce, but they can also thrive. As counsellor and community worker Bangambiki Habyarimana says, "Sometimes divorce is the best thing that can happen to marriage." Your kids don't know that now. They can't. But they will.

———————

You can see these positive and negative effects in the following quotes from famous children of broken marriages:

"E.T. began with me trying to write a story about my parents' divorce."

— STEVEN SPIELBERG

"My parents' divorce left me with a lot of sadness and pain, and acting, and especially humour, was my way of dealing with that."

— JENNIFER ANISTON

"My parents' divorce made an important change in my life. It affected me. After that, when I couldn't play Wimbledon, it was tough. For one month, I was outside the world."

— RAFAEL NADAL

A famous director, a beloved actress, a legendary tennis player. All children of divorce. All individuals who have reached the top of their professions by channelling their experiences in productive, creative ways that have given pleasure and excitement to the rest of us.

In almost no scenario is divorce easy on kids. It creates pain, turmoil, complexity, and confusion. But it can also lead to healing in all sorts of unexpected ways, and kids, being the amazing creatures they are, can surprise you with the ways in which they turn that difficulty into wonderful things. Most important is that you're there for them during their journey, providing shelter from the storm, so that they can emerge into the sunlight in surprising and delightful ways.

My Split Through My Daughter's Eyes

I asked my kids if they would be willing to contribute to this book. I told them there was no pressure, but if they wanted to, they could write, in their own words, what the hardest parts of Mommy and Daddy splitting up have been, and — this was wishful thinking on my part — if there was anything positive about the experience. Dustin and Cory declined my request, but Alisha insisted. Actually, she demanded a whole chapter. I told her to just write as much as she wanted. So, if you don't mind, I'd like to give her the last word in this chapter. Here's what she wrote, with no editing from me:

> I think that the hardest part of them breaking up was when I first found out about it. Mostly because I didn't know how to respond when I heard. Now I am used to the routine because it's been about five years.

If there is anything that I'm happy about because of their breaking up, it would probably be that they don't really fight anymore, which leads me into the next thing. I am very proud of my parents because I know a lot of people whose parents are divorced and fight whenever they see each other. But, as far as I know, my parents are good friends, they rarely fight (and if they ever do, it's just a small argument), and they split their time fairly with us.

I was kind of scared when I first heard that they were going to split up. I thought that maybe I would never get to see my dad again. I never told anyone though. At first my dad moved in with his parents. We would sleep over only one day a week, sometimes he would stop by at our house to drop off something, but that didn't happen often. I was not used to this at all, and I was scared that one day he might move to another country on the other side of the world and never come visit us or call us, then forget about us.

Now I know that would never happen.

If I had to give advice to other parents who are going through a breakup to make it easier for the kids, I would say not to fight (at least not in front of the kids). Try to be kind to each other and don't get your children involved in any discord that goes on between the two of you.

That is all I have to say.

Ten Questions: My Friend and Linemate Andy

What were the biggest mistakes you made with your kids during your split, and how have you addressed them?
Initially, I think the biggest mistake I made was not spending as much time as I should have with the kids when the separation first happened. Because of the volatility with my ex, coupled with the novelty of a new relationship, I didn't set aside enough quality time with my kids. That changed, but it's important to ensure one makes every effort to spend as much time — proper time — with the kids. Even taking them away somewhere close to home would have been a good idea.

I also wish I'd discussed the situation more explicitly with them, especially the older ones. It's so difficult for children to understand exactly what's occurring, and there's a ton of emotional upheaval on all sides. We should have given them more reassurance, that I and their mom still loved them just the same and that things would be all right. I also think that would have offset some of the negative talk that my ex engaged in about me. I didn't retaliate, but I also didn't do enough to ensure my kids didn't internalize negative and/or untruthful things she was saying.

Afterwards, I think I should have done more to reassure my kids that they were still the most important people in my life, in particular more important than my new partner. I know now that, when a split happens, kids naturally fear they are no longer the biggest priority in your life, and there is a tendency for them to have a confirmatory bias when they see you doing things, or agreeing with, your new partner instead of them.

I also think it's good to have set custody arrangements, with some flexibility for exceptional circumstances. Having set days establishes a routine and provides a sense of normalcy. I don't recommend having an open-door policy at both households, regardless of whether you get along. Boundaries are important.

What's been your greatest challenge?
Rebuilding my relationship with my kids. After the separation, I didn't spend much time with them initially. In addition to my not being around every day, they were also left to the negative influence of my ex. If I could have a do-over, I'd make the extra effort to spend time with the kids.

Can you describe your lowest or hardest moments with your kids?
My lowest moment was when I realized my kids had suffered emotionally as a result of my not having handled things well with them.

How about moments when you saw light at the end of the tunnel?
Things started normalizing once there was a regular schedule between the two households and I moved closer to them. The kids started living with me part-time, and they began to interact better with my girlfriend. They were also getting a bit older, which helped.

In your view, what do kids need most from their dad during or after a breakup?
I think what kids need most from their dads is stability. They need to feel like their lives are going on as usual, and there is a sense of normalcy and regularity. Their lives have been changed forever. So spending quality time with them, maintaining their usual routines, trying to live close to them if possible, continuing with the same activities, being calm in answering their questions, talking openly and honestly with them — all these things will help with the psychological adjustment.

How much emotion did you show your kids with regard to your split? Where do you stand on how much "real" they should see versus how much they should be protected?
I didn't show much emotion at all. I believed it was important to remain calm and not to involve my kids in any of the issues between their parents. I think that was even more important given my ex's frame of mind at the time.

That said, I think it's important to respond to negative things your ex may say about you. While it's noble to take the high road, I think it's also important to address, in a careful, constructive manner, anything that has been said that may affect how your kids feel about you. I didn't bad-mouth my ex. I think my kids recognized and appreciated the level of respect I tried to maintain regardless of what she did.

What would you say are the key hurdles to get over as a family before kids can start adjusting to the new normal?
Peace with your ex; no bad-mouthing. If kids keep hearing one or both spouses bash the other, it will keep them trapped in conflict.

Routine is important to bring about a sense of normalcy — to say that life goes on and it's not chaos, there is structure.

A good relationship with your new partner. If the kids don't bond with the new partner, things will never be normal. There will always be resentment. Quality time with the new partner is essential. Have her go out with the kids and treat them to a good time, with and without you present.

How do you handle the practical issues of two households?
There is no science here. I think it's very important to speak with the ex and establish a routine so that the kids know what to expect, and it's important to have uniform rules as much as possible. I managed to do well with it by having a set routine but allowing flexibility as well. There will be times where you have to deviate from the set schedule, and there will be times where your ex will request an indulgence. Allow for that to the extent it's reasonable; don't make a mountain out of a molehill.

What are your top three pieces of advice to other dads for maintaining a loving and healthy relationship with their kids after a split?
One, quality time! Especially right after the separation. As much as there may be a pull to spend time with your new partner, make sure you put your kids first. Also, hug them. Stay up and hang

out together — watch TV, play video games, anything. Do the things they like.

Two, routine. Routine helps things keep going as they always have — school, activities, visits to friends and family. Set scheduled time with you and with your ex.

Three, have a good relationship with your ex. It's important to show kids that even though things didn't work out, there is a base level of respect and cooperation. Model for them how to deal with conflict. Don't let them get caught in unfair and unnecessary crossfire.

3

Processing Your Guilt

As any parent knows, from the moment your kids are born, you spend most of your waking hours hoping nothing bad will happen to them. During a split, you see pain and confusion in their innocent eyes — a situation so unjust that you want to flog yourself. They ask the inevitable questions — "If you love us so much, then why did you and Mommy break up?" — over and over, and the answers you come up with are so maddeningly useless that you can't stand hearing yourself talk. Friends quote you the divorce rate and remind you that you aren't the first or the last couple to break up. People who have gone through a breakup tell you, "Don't worry, you get used to not seeing your kids every day." You want to punch these people in the nose. Others, less prone to sugarcoating things, tell you their son or daughter barely spoke to them for a couple of years after the breakup, but then they got older and, over time, things started to improve. You want to punch these people too. Nothing salves the guilt. You carry it around day and night.

An essential part of the journey through divorce is to make sense of, and figure out how to process, the guilt that threatens to engulf you. Immediately after you tell your kids the news that is going to shatter their existence, the guilt takes root inside and starts to spread. On most days, you privately ask for more of it, because you're convinced you deserve to feel all this and more for what you're making your kids go through. You own the heck out of it. But the guilt is not useful if it is only going to drown you. It cannot be shed and it should not be ignored. It needs to be faced, understood, and absorbed in a way that will not swamp your spirit. Guilt is the toughest part of the psychological and emotional road you are on. Let's talk about why you want to hold onto it so badly, and the reasons you need to be able to, at least intermittently, let it go.

For the sake of solidarity, here's a sampling of my most guilt-laced moments, in no particular order.

- Alisha's voice on the phone on one of the kids' nights with my ex soon after the split, barely audible, breaking softly, asking me why I couldn't come tuck her in.
- Driving Cory to school one morning and hearing him say to his best friend, "My mommy and daddy broke up, and I don't really know what to do. I was wondering if I could talk to you about it." I wanted to ask the boys if I could drop them off at the corner so that I could drive myself into the nearest lamppost.
- A month after the breakup, on a March evening when the temperature in Toronto was still below zero, Dustin insisting on playing baseball with me at the cul-de-sac where we'd always played, in an obvious and frantic desire to cling to an activity that felt normal. In our winter coats and hats, I threw balls to him and he hit them. Every swing he took was so angry and violent it made me want to cry. My fingers were numb after twenty minutes, but we kept going. After forty minutes, it was so dark we could barely see. When I told him we had to go inside, he wasn't so much mad as desperate. In his eyes I could read as clear as day what he was really saying: *Please, Daddy, can't we just keep playing?* I wanted to tear myself limb from limb.

- Any time I dropped the kids back at the house. The looks on their faces as I said goodbye. The sound of the door closing. The feeling of walking down the front path, the one I'd shovelled a hundred times, toward my car. All of the energy and light rushing out of me. Getting in the car and trying to drive around the corner fast enough so the kids wouldn't have to see me cry. All the sequential acts of purposely going away from my kids. How I hated myself.

- Having to say things like, "Well, um, we can't tonight because it's Mommy's night, and, um, it wouldn't be fair to her to … change the schedule" — all versions of which felt tantamount to saying, "Sorry, but you aren't as important to me as my own happiness. Well, no, that's not it, you actually *are* my happiness, it's just that it was really hard living with Mommy for a bunch of reasons you don't understand and won't for, like, twenty years, so I've decided it's better to do this addition-by-subtraction thing, if you get what I mean, which you don't. Anyway, your tiny heart is just collateral damage, and by the way, you and your relationships are probably screwed up for life because of the way you keep perceiving me demonstrating my rejection of you, even though what you don't understand is that I'm dying every hour I don't see you. We good?"

You may have noted that the moment when I told my kids their mommy and I were breaking up is not part of this list. That moment involved many different emotions, including tremendous sadness, but not guilt. I knew in my heart I was doing the right thing, for them and for us as a family, despite the heartbreak of watching them have to deal with it.

The hardest part was that, even if I believed the decision to split was right, and that the children would be better off eventually, "eventually" was a long way off, and it seemed impossible to envision the bridge between then and now. In my mind, it looked like a bridge consisting less of solid planks than of broken spaces for my kids to fall through. It's due to creating such tumult in one's kids' lives that the guilt can be so inundating at times. You can feel with every fibre that the breakup is the lesser of two evils, but you've had to crush your children's hearts to achieve that goal, which doesn't feel like a goal as much as a selfish concession.

I kept thinking of a song from one of my favourite musicals, *Miss Saigon*: "I'd Give My Life for You." The protagonist sings it to her infant son as an apology for the circumstances into which she's brought him. In her case, those circumstances are having had to become a prostitute at a bar in Saigon after her parents were killed in the Vietnam War. Clearly this situation is not parallel to a separation between a middle-class couple living in Toronto. Still, the guilt toward my kids felt similar. They hadn't asked to be born, and they hadn't asked for this. Lugging the guilt around was like wearing a coat of little scalpels.

Many dads refer to the personal shame of their relationship having failed. As psychologist Andrew Shaul says, "One of the most common issues I see with dads having gone through a split is that embarrassing feeling of 'I wrecked my family and my children.' Even though on one level they may be blaming the ex, on another they may be thinking, 'What's wrong with me?'"

Though I was obviously surprised that my relationship failed, insofar as one doesn't go into a marriage expecting that it will end, my guilt was based on how many other people I felt I was letting down. The first, obviously, were my kids. Next were my parents. They'd given me a life, a home, an education, and a social life. They'd given me access to opportunities, friends, sports, trips, and everything a child could ask for. They'd worked for decades to make life as positive as it could be for me. Now all they wanted to do was sit back and enjoy retirement together while spending every second they could with their grandchildren. After everything they'd done for me, I had repaid them by throwing their plan into disarray, including complicating that grandkid time. My kids were the greatest gift I ever gave them, and now I was reneging on that gift in the worst possible way. I felt cruel.

My Split Through My Parents' Eyes

Just as I asked my kids if they wanted to talk about their experience of the breakup, I also asked my parents. During the three years I lived with them after my split, I saw them ripped apart day after day by my struggle. Just as I was dying inside because of my own kids' pain, I knew they were dying inside because of mine. I asked them to tell me the three most difficult things they experienced regarding my split and the top three positive outcomes, if any. Here's what they wrote:

> Hi, SB [they call me Sonny Boy because that's what my late maternal grandmother called me — you have to imagine it being said with a Yiddish accent]. This was a really difficult exercise. We tried to be very honest as you asked, as painful as that was. We hope this is helpful and that our responses land well with you. Lots of love, Mom and Dad

Hardest Things

The hardest thing by far was watching the effects on the kids. I can still hear Dustin screaming, "I don't want to be here! I hate it here! I want to go home!" It killed us. Cory's reactions and behaviours were so painful to watch, both because of what we knew he was going through and the equal pain of watching how it was affecting you. We felt such deep distress, and so helpless.

The loss of the family unit and the extended family as we had come to know it was so sudden, and left us feeling disconnected. Where do we go to see the kids? Will family dinners, birthdays, etc. ever be the same? How do we now behave, and connect, with the family and friends on your now ex's side? What is our relationship with her going to be?

What followed was like a nightmare that kept repeating over and over, and which we didn't know how to resolve.

Our fear for you was constant. We knew how much you love your kids and how much you love being a dad. We were frightened the emotional and financial challenges might overwhelm you. We wanted to be there to support you, but we often felt at a loss as to how.

Positive Outcomes

We got our son back! Over the years, you had changed and withdrawn from us. We felt we had lost who you had been. As you settled into being a single dad, you returned to the person we knew you to be.

The stress in our family time was gone. We recognized how much of it there had been behind the scenes for you, and for how long. Our dinners and vacation time were now lighthearted, uncomplicated, and fun.

We developed an even greater sense of the importance of our connection with our grandkids. More than ever, we felt the desire to provide a safe, calm, loving environment for them. Through the toughest period, we felt we grew closer to them.

Once I started living with my parents, I felt even guiltier. Parents raise you to be strong, independent, and, they hope, self-sufficient. Now here I was, living under their roof again, eating their food, using their stuff, disturbing their lives. I felt like a screw-up. Not so much because my marriage had ended, but for complicating the peace and simplicity my parents had worked so hard to earn, and for making so heavy this period of their lives that was meant to be the lightest.

I'd made things almost indescribably difficult for them overnight — asking them to get up early to take the kids to school because, due to distance, I couldn't get to work and get the kids to school at the same time; throwing them into a harsh and hostile dynamic between me and my ex; making them face the rest of their years having to now answer the question "How's I.J.?" with the answer "He's divorced."

When the kids would sleep over, that guilt would multiply by, oh, about a quintillion percent. There were two single beds in "my room," so two of the three kids would sleep on those, and the other either on the couch in the main room or the kind-of sofa in the office. Alisha would usually sleep in the office, with me on the floor next to her. She would ask me to cover the light from the external drive attached to the computer, which would blink and scare her. My sons would fight about who got to sleep in which bed, since here they didn't have their own rooms like they did at what they called "home," which tore my heart to pieces every time they said it. They would complain about having to get up half an hour earlier to get to school. On most days, when I would get up at 5:30 to start making their lunches for school that day, I would see my mom, dad, or both already up and doing it for me, so I could get some extra minutes of sleep. They were terrified at how wrecked I looked. I was overwhelmed with guilt at their unending love and generosity.

I felt additional guilt at what I imagined would be the unavoidable implosion of my kids' extended world of cousins, aunts, uncles, and others. At a time when they would need all the support they could get, I felt I was fracturing that bedrock of extended family. It's important to keep that extended system alive, especially because, as London psychotherapist Dipti Shah says, "With the huge amount of stress kids experience figuring out how to suddenly exist in two separate homes, they often benefit from having some neutral space." Just as your kids will benefit from seeing that the stuff of their daily lives remains intact, it will also help them to see that the broader scope of those lives remains the same, including family events, holiday parties, celebratory dinners, weddings, baby namings, and so on. "When the split affects wider family systems," advises Shah, "the kids are left with another loss, of separation from the extended family resource."

You and your ex may both feel the urge to put up family fences. But, warns Shah, the kids are already experiencing the splintering of their immediate family, so the wider you can make their familial safety net, the more support they will have. In other words, don't try to position your family over your ex's. Half the time, my kids barely knew which side of the family a given person was on; they just knew them as family. Encourage time spent with the other side of the family just as you would have done before. Avoid saying negative things about your ex's family members, for example, "They aren't my cousins anymore." The more people who love and care for your kids, the better. Your children staying close to relatives on your ex's side doesn't tip any invisible scale in her favour. It just creates a wider safety net of love and warmth for your kids.

———————

The guilt might hurt so much that you pledge never to do anything ever again to make your kids feel unease. So you overcompensate by ceasing to be a parent and instead become a full-time enjoyment giver or difficulty remover. Remember that what your kids need from you most is for you just to be their dad, who listens to them, has fun with them, and also provides rules and boundaries.

My friend Gord told me this story about how guilt impacted his relationship with his daughter:

> From the moment I made the decision to split with my now ex-wife, I was racked with guilt about our daughter (let's call her B.), and how I would have to make up for the fact that I was turning her world upside down. This guilt impaired my judgment.
>
> In general, I would avoid asking her to do the normal things expected of a kid — clean up after herself, help with chores, be a productive member of the house. And on the other side of the coin, because I now wasn't living with her full-time, I turned the time I did have with her into party time. We ate out a lot, went to movies. I bought her new stuff: clothes, shoes, the latest gadgets. I didn't enforce rules. Once we were on vacation in Mexico, and she and a friend stayed out late and went into a local town. She was too young to have that freedom, and even

though I was angry with her, I found it hard to discipline her because I was afraid she'd be mad at me. I'd lost perspective about my role.

I expected B. to be angry with me that her home situation had changed because of my decision to split from her mom. It was a difficult time for my ex-wife, and the first few months after the split were a roller coaster of outbursts, anger, sadness, and some horrendously difficult confrontations. I was the bad guy, and yet I observed B. moving easily between her mom and me, between our separate locations, and between our two lives. There was never a harsh word from her, never a sarcastic barb thrown my way. She seemed as normal as a kid could be.

Subconsciously, the issue of my guilt was always lurking. I couldn't erase or ease it. I see now that all of my attempts to be lenient, and my endlessly giving B. gifts or money, were ways to try to deal with this guilt. It started with being generous in small, unnecessary ways, then kept growing. Eventually I realized I was not being a good parent as much as I was trying to be a good friend, so as not to alienate her.

I wish I had been smart enough to figure this out on my own, but it took someone with an outside view to help me understand that my guilt was misguided, that B. loved me for just being her dad, and that she needed me to be a true parent, including setting guidelines or giving advice she might not like.

The guilt does get easier to manage, slowly. As they say, time heals. It's taken over twenty years for me to realize how many mistakes I made with B. I still make some of them. For instance, I still cling to the thought that I have to soften the message if it isn't a positive one, for fear that B. may not like me. As you can see, I'm still working on it!

As Gord's story illustrates, your guilt can cause you to overcompensate in unhealthy ways. It can also lead you to make bad decisions that may not be good for your kids. For instance, you might want to show your ex a sense of compassion but allow it to manifest in the wrong kind of way. The following story is from my friend Raj.

> The biggest mistake I made was a result of my guilt. I knew my ex was ill-equipped for raising a child single-handedly, but I thought leaving my daughter with her would give her purpose. I also thought I could still be a strong and supportive presence even living apart. It was okay for a while, but in the long run, this proved a massive miscalculation. My daughter is troubled and struggling today, and I will always regret not having fought for her to live with me.
>
> At the time I couldn't imagine the guilt of both [leaving] my wife and then also taking her daughter away.... [This resulted in me] ... making the wrong decision. I took my daughter every weekend for ten years, even though her mom moved her an hour north of Toronto three months after we separated, which effectively ended any chance I had to be a more regular presence and influence. Despite trying to stay as involved as I could, I wasn't able to offset the bad habits and counter the darkness that my ex instilled in her.
>
> My ex is not a bad person, but she has her own issues and hasn't been able to set them aside or shelter my daughter from the effects. So if I had to do anything differently, I would have made decisions based on what was best for my daughter — not based on my guilt.

The guilt you feel isn't going to be departing any time soon, but there are things you can do to manage it. Here are six:

- **Write about it.** I don't want to get all writerly on you, but the simplest way for anyone to process their emotions on the most basic level is to get them out. To that end, try keeping a daily journal. Write down what you're feeling. This isn't for any purpose other than to provide a conduit for a lot of dark and heavy emotions accumulating inside you. The more space you allow them to occupy, the higher your risk of lashing out. Give yourself an outlet.

- **Compartmentalize it.** The line between showing your kids real emotions and demonstrating strength and resolve is a delicate one. Though I wouldn't advise you to suppress your feelings in general, I do think you ought to do so when with your kids. Do deal with it, but deal with it away from them. The more you wear your guilt on your sleeve, the more confusing the situation is for your kids, because they may think you not only feel bad about the grief they're feeling, which is appropriate, but you also perhaps question your decision, which is not appropriate. This leads me to my next suggestion on how to handle your guilt.

- **Be honest with your kids about it.** You do feel bad. You feel really bad. Don't be afraid to say this to your kids, but say it without conveying messages you don't intend. "I'm sorry for the pain this is causing you" is a different message from "I'm sorry Mommy and I broke up." You're not sorry for that, because it was a difficult and courageous decision made for their ultimate benefit. Help your kids understand that you're hurting for them but still convinced about your decision, because grasping this is an important step in their emotional passage.

- **Fight it.** "The hardest thing about depression," said Pete Wentz, member of the American band Fall Out Boy, "is that it is addictive. It begins to feel uncomfortable not to be depressed. You feel guilty for feeling happy."

    The guilt you feel about the effect of your marriage breakup on your kids is huge, and because of this, it can be debilitating if you resign yourself to it. You may not recognize how much your guilt is manifesting in your physical and mental self. If your kids see you walking around as though you're in quicksand, your behaviour won't give them much hope. Grab a branch and pull yourself out, not so much so you can see the light, but so they can.

"There are two kinds of guilt," writes author Sabaa Tahir, "the kind that drowns you until you're useless, and the kind that fires your soul to purpose." Don't show your kids that you're drowning in your guilt, even if on the inside it feels like you are. Show them fire and purpose. Again, if you feel you're in crisis, please seek professional help right away.

- **Process it with those who know you best and care for you most.** The deeper and more acute the emotion you feel, the more you need someone who really knows you to be able to help you process it. You can try for hours or days to work through the guilt on your own and come up empty, yet a few words from someone who genuinely cares for you can be transformative. There have been many moments since I have been with my partner, Fulvia, when I have broken down, overwhelmed by a wave of sorrow, and an equal number in which she has provided a loving gesture, a few words of calm reassurance, or a tender insight to slowly bring me back and move me forward. This positive effect isn't a magic trick. It's the result of sincere, generous, and deeply compassionate love. (For more on the importance of connecting with friends and family, see Chapter 8.)

- **Embrace it.** Andrew Shaul said something to me that I found brilliant: Working through guilt isn't the same as trying to get rid of it. The idea doesn't seem an intuitive one, but it's true. "Sometimes," he said, "what seems to help is accepting the guilt rather than trying to eliminate it. You got married with the best of intentions, but here you are:

you're splitting, and you have kids who are hurting from the decision, so naturally you have guilt. Instead of fighting it, try to process it as a natural consequence. You can look at it as a terrible thing you need to get rid of or an understandable by-product of the decision, which you need to adjust to and reduce your suffering from."

I found this insight to be both completely surprising and totally sensible. You have to face it and embrace it.

I just made up that expression. I'm going with it.

My friend Tracie, who had gone through a breakup a few months before I did, said this to me: "When you tell your kids, it's going to be the worst day of your life. But if it's the right thing to do, you'll get through it, and so will they." She was certainly right about the first part. I've relived that awful moment in my mind over and over: calling the kids into the basement and telling them, in some sequence of awkward and incoherent words I can't remember or don't want to, that Mommy and Daddy were breaking up. Dustin, ten at the time, going quiet and starting to play with a toy on the carpet. Alisha, five, starting to weep quietly, ripping my heart into a thousand pieces. Cory, eight, taking Alisha in his arms and telling her she would be okay. The scene was surreal, the guilt incalculable. I stood outside myself asking how I could ruin my children's lives so callously. But it was the moment that was necessary from which to move on — to start to move on — as a family.

You didn't fail your kids. You did something extremely tough and really brave, for the sake of their happiness and health. "Divorce isn't such a tragedy," wrote author Jennifer Weiner. "A tragedy's staying in an unhappy marriage, teaching your children the wrong things about love." I know that the guilt you feel is horrendous and heavy. But you will learn how to absorb and accept it as a natural part of a good decision made for the right reasons, and your kids, over time, will show you that they understand.

———————

Ten Questions: My Friend Chad

What were the biggest mistakes you made with your kids during your split, and how have you addressed them?
I think my ex and I did a pretty admirable job of co-parenting our daughter, including taking holidays together. If I made any mistake, it wasn't due to the divorce — it was moving on to the next (wrong) relationship and letting that person influence the parental relationship between me and my ex.

What's been your greatest challenge?
Having to move farther away from my daughter for my job — from the same city as her to twelve hundred miles away — the subsequent fight for custody that entailed, and ultimately not being with her as often as I would have liked. I've tried to handle it by making the best possible life I can, staying in hers as much as she will allow, and, when we're together, being totally present with her so that we have amazing times and create lasting memories.

Can you describe your lowest or hardest moments with your daughter?
The hardest thing by far was having to leave her after being the primary parent for the first seven years of her life. The memory of her screams as I left the house to fly to another city still breaks my heart.

How about moments when you saw light at the end of the tunnel?
Never had darkness (other than the move), so there was never a light needed. Once I lost custody, it wasn't about light; it was about adjusting.

In your view, what do kids need most from their dad during or after a breakup?
Love. A father's love is powerful, and kids need it. If there's one thing a father needs to do, it's to make sure not to put down the kids' mother. She's important to the children. Don't bring too many dates around either.

How much emotion did you show your kids with regard to your split? Where do you stand on how much "real" they should see versus how much they should be protected?
They need to know enough to help them learn from the experiences and failures of their parents, but they don't need to know the details.

What would you say are the key hurdles to get over as a family before kids can start adjusting to the new normal?
The parents need to establish what the new normal will be. Once it's figured out and the parents are living it, the kids will adjust. My daughter was young, so it was easier.

How do you handle the practical issues of two households?
We did quite well because we kept up communication. At handoff times, we would always talk and update each other. We did well at being in the same room together because we agreed to put our daughter first.

What are your top three pieces of advice to other dads for maintaining a loving and healthy relationship with their kids after a split?
One, love them as though nothing has changed, so they know not to blame themselves.

Two, talk to them. Talk *with* them. Always be communicating. They need to know you're always there, interested in what they're thinking and feeling, and ready to listen.

Three, never bad-mouth their mom or do things you know will cause rifts in the family dynamic. One thing that doesn't change is that the two of you are still their parents together, and you always will be.

And here's an extra: don't be just Disneyland Dad, giving them nothing but fun and games and then handing them back to their mom for rules and discipline. You still need to do all the things a parent is supposed to do.

4

Communicating with Your Ex

The Moving Finger writes; and, having writ,
Moves on: nor all thy Piety nor Wit
Shall lure it back to cancel half a Line,
Nor all thy Tears wash out a Word of it.

— Omar Khayyám

The person you called your partner is now the person you call your ex. Whether you did the leaving, were the one who was left, or the two of you made the decision to split simultaneously, you were on a journey together, and now you're … well, you still are on a journey, whether you like it or not. Just a different one. While in one sense you're just as tied together as you were before, you suddenly have a strange new task, which is to become, in the ideal scenario, friends, but, at minimum, functional co-parents. To say the process of learning to co-manage your kids' lives in this scenario is going to take some time is like saying it's a little hard to balance a pencil on its tip.

For starters, a couple of assumptions you may have held are likely being disabused. For example, you may have harboured the fantasy that, once apart, you and your ex would magically get along better. That may be the case at some point, but you're still the same people you were before, so you're likely to have the same kinds of disagreements and cause each other the same types of frustrations.

During the first weeks and months after the split, every conversation is a potential minefield, with emotions swinging between hot and seething. Your most challenging task in this period is to find that inner Zen when it seems impossible to access. In even the most cordial split, wires are constantly being tripped. And, again, if your personalities were incompatible during the partnership, guess what? They still are — and now chances are, one or both of you are plenty angry too.

For the sake of your kids — and I'll be repeating this approximately two dozen times in this chapter — you have to get along. Nothing predicts more harmful outcomes for kids than their parents acting nasty to each other. The more anxiety your kids feel at witnessing or becoming triangulated in fighting between you and your ex, the worse they can be expected to fare. At times you'll need to use every ounce of willpower and composure in your body to get along with your ex. Yet you must. Let's talk about how to traverse the journey from partners to co-parents, why it's so important to steer your way through the different phases with grace, compassion, and resolve, and why this effort, though sometimes Herculean, will make all the difference to your kids.

———————

Kids are resilient — often more than we think. Make no mistake, divorce sucks for them, and sucks big time. But it doesn't have to be all bad. Says therapist Lindsey Jay Walsh, "Kids usually map onto the world around them pretty well. Especially if they feel loved and supported, they can adapt. If there is chaos in the family, there will likely be chaos in the child." Translation: If you and your ex make the effort to get along, your kids can make positive strides faster. "Kids seem to be able to find a new normal much faster than adults," says Walsh, "particularly if Mom and Dad manage to communicate." You're going to hear that until you're sick of it: everything will work out … *if Mom and Dad manage to communicate.*

The day after I told our kids their mom and I were splitting up, I was shocked when Dustin and Cory marched into the kitchen and presented a custody schedule they'd designed. It was an unbearably sweet calendar scrawled in crayon. It made me feel even deeper love for them, and even guiltier than I already did. Yet it also showed me a glimpse of their astounding capacity to adjust and the importance of unity between me and my ex, or at least the appearance of it. While things behind the scenes were a hot mess, what my kids had witnessed was an announcement that, though horrible, had been delivered calmly and, at least on the surface, jointly. It seemed this had allowed them to react with a similar kind of solidarity. I prayed we could continue along that road. We couldn't, as most people can't, do so, at least not entirely, but the lesson was stark.

I know what you might be saying right now: "I get that it's important to try to get along. But you have no idea how she presses my buttons." First of all, yes I do. And I don't care. You press her buttons too. As I said, this part is very simple: you need to get along. "Do whatever you have to do to cultivate a friendship with your ex," says family counsellor and author Alyson Schafer. "Suck it up and be adults. Be respectful. Be friendly. Be united. Kids don't know how to have loyalty to one parent." In fact, you'd better learn how to get along for your own sanity, because you and your ex are going to be co-parents for the rest of your lives. You may be living apart, but you and she are still going to have to make decisions together for years to come.

Says Portland counsellor Yshai Boussi, "It's often surprising how much communication is involved between parents after a split." That's true. You will have innumerable conversations in which you need to ask stuff of each other. Your instincts during these conversations may often be driven by negative feelings or biases conditioned over time. Try to resist these automatic responses; maintain a firm eye on the goal of mutual problem solving instead. Try not to blame ("I told her a million times to pack that"), to generalize ("She's always disorganized"), to be sarcastic ("What a surprise she had a problem with the lunch I packed you"), to sound exasperated ("She drives me crazy"), or to be comparing ("She should have Scotch tape like I do"). Do be diplomatic, neutral, compassionate, and focused on your kids' needs rather than your ex's flaws.

Sometimes your attitude toward your ex will feel entirely negative. She'll often feel that way about you too. Neither of you is as bad as you seem to the other. You're both just going through something really hard. If you allow yourself to get to the place where you have nothing but bad thoughts about her, you will transmit that feeling to your kids, even if you think you aren't. (Want to know three things that are true? They know more than you think. They hear more than you think. And they understand more than you think.) You may be carrying a lot of stuff inside that you didn't say when you were together that you now not only feel at liberty to say, but, especially in certain moments, would really, really like to say. Don't. Nothing good will come of it.

This is a death you're mourning — the death of your family structure — and grief brings with it many complicated emotions. Again, likely the most frequent and irrepressible of these will be the fault-finding impulse. I would like you to promise me that you will try to push it back down when it rears its ugly head. There are three reasons you should hold back from blaming your ex for everything :

- **It will become exhausting.** Practise asking yourself what role you may have played in a given situation. Not because I want you to figure out who was at fault, but because this is a healthy and mature practice. It's arguably an even more important habit after your split than it was before. It will help to stop the resentment you're already feeling from escalating in a way that can paralyze you from making good decisions.
- **It sets a bad example.** Blaming your ex for everything is not a good way to model conflict resolution to your kids. If they witness you always claiming that things are their mom's fault, this will teach them to point fingers too.
- **It doesn't make sense.** Mathematically speaking, how could everything be her fault? Or yours, for that matter? You're both human beings. Impressive species, sure, but pretty flawed.

An exercise I've found useful is to reframe blame-type thoughts or statements before I fall prey to them. For example, in certain circumstances I might want to say, "No, I don't know why Mommy isn't coming to basketball today. I would never miss one of your games." A better message would be, "Mommy works really hard all week and does a lot more for you guys than you realize. She might just be tired." Or I might hear these kinds of words forming in my head: "We have a late fine at the library? Mommy told me three times she was going to drop off the book. You can see why she drove me nuts." A good alternative would be, "It looks like Mommy and I had a miscommunication, but don't worry, we'll figure it out."

What's that? You're asking me what about when something *is* her fault? Then let me ask you back: What if it is? What difference does that make to your kids? It doesn't matter whether they know who misplaced the sneakers, forgot the address to the birthday party, or packed the wrong snack. A more powerful message to send to them is that you and your ex are dealing with things together, in a fair and equitable manner, which means sharing credit in the good situations and sharing responsibility in the bad. My friend Afrom advises, "Despite your own pain, try to find the strength to empathize with your ex, and always keep in mind what's best for the kids in the long run instead of your personal feelings in the moment. This is a traumatic experience for both of you, and the effort to be mutually understanding will help everyone. Don't put your kids in the middle. Be bigger."

If you don't need any other reason to get along with your ex, here's a reminder of the only one you really need to know, in the words of Toronto psychologist Andrew Shaul: "The biggest predictor of how kids handle separation or divorce is usually how the parents get along. So do the work. You left the marriage. You've already made that point. Now, take the high road. Having held your tongue is going to feel much better than being able to say 'I got my digs in.'" I could spend the rest of this book describing studies that show correlations between divorced parents' ability to get along and their kids' outcomes, from emotional to behavioural, social to academic. In short, how the two of you interact affects everything in your kids' lives, today, tomorrow, and, most likely, always.

———————

Speaking positively about your ex includes not trashing the relationship you two had in front of your kids. Right now you may feel miserable about not only the current situation but everything that came before, the way gathering storm clouds may obscure a previously clear and sunny sky. Inadvertently conveying this to your children is hazardous for one very important reason: if they come to believe that you resent the relationship that produced them, what do you think they'll believe about how you feel toward them? The relationship with your ex ended at a certain point, for certain reasons. It's okay to be (mostly) honest about that. But don't drag down the rest of the relationship.

When your kids talk about, for example, the surprise birthday party your ex threw for you, you can say something like, "Yeah, well, that was a long time ago," or you can say, "That was really fun, she totally got me." You're not compromising your dignity by choosing to say the latter. You're showing your kids that you honour the union that created them. Acknowledging the good times will ease their hurt. Acting as though the past was only bad will make them question their own worth in your eyes.

My friend Gary calls this the issue of "memory management." Below is what he wrote about it, exactly as he sent it to me. I haven't edited a word because I find it reads almost like a free verse poem, as well as the right kind of prescription for how to uphold the memory of something while still moving forward from it.

> How do you retain the fondness of a shared memory
> without colouring it with the emotion of your current
> circumstances?
> At some point you have to sort through the photos and
> videos amassed over the years
> All of a sudden it becomes terribly difficult to experience
> a given moment
> captured in the way you did before
> The danger is that if we poison our memories with emo-
> tion surrounding the separation

then we risk seeing the whole marriage through the
same lens
It is a short extrapolation to see your time together as
a waste
And next comes blame, anger, and resentment
Keep the fondness of your life alive — especially for your
children

I keep these words close as a kind of mantra. Whenever I experience a frustrating moment with my ex that might prompt me to make a negative comment about the past, I read them over and they remind me to behave respectfully, for the sake of my children. It's a good bet that things will come up all the time that remind you why the relationship with your ex didn't work. Resist the need to cite these things to your kids as a way of justifying the split. They don't need justification; they just need love. The rest they'll figure out in time.

In the same vein, when you find a new relationship that makes you feel the things you want to feel, allow the positive aspects of that relationship to become visible to your kids through the organic changes they will see in you. Don't use the happiness you are feeling in your new relationship as an excuse for making unfavourable comments about your ex. (For more on new relationships, see Chapter 10.)

It didn't take me long after meeting Fulvia to recognize that she was my ideal partner. She made me feel everything I had ever dreamed of feeling, and this sensation filled me day and night. Naturally, many of the positives in our relationship stood in contrast to the negatives in my previous one. At times, I felt the urge to point out these differences to my kids. Then a friend who had gone through a split told me, "You don't have to tell your kids how happy you are. They'll see it. If they ask why, tell them. Describe the things about her that you find so wonderful. Talk honestly about the positives of that relationship without having to talk smack about the other one. It's the biggest favour you can do for them."

I really appreciated this advice. You can celebrate all that is joyful and fulfilling about the new relationship without vilifying the previous one. I love to talk about Fulvia and all of the qualities that make me so crazy about her. She does things every day that make me fall in love with her again and again. Allowing my kids to discover this in a natural and spontaneous way makes sense. I want them to see my happiness and understand the reasons for it — including why it makes me a better dad — while letting them feel secure about the relationship they came from.

Not denigrating the relationship you had with your ex includes not speaking badly of the place in which that relationship occurred. That's the home where your kids have grown up, the place where they have formed their memories. It's critical that, even though in your mind and heart you may be moving on, you try not to demonstrate emotional detachment from memories built in the space you shared together.

My kids and my ex and I lived in the same house together for over a decade. It was the only home my children knew prior to my moving in with my parents and then finally getting my own apartment. I wanted my new place to become their second home, equivalent in comfort and warmth to the first. But this takes time. Once I got my apartment, when the kids would talk about the other home — maybe how comfortable their beds were, or how fun the crawl space was to explore, or how great the backyard was — I had an urge to downplay their positive comments, because I wanted them to love their home with *me*. At first they would call my former matrimonial house "home" and my new place "the apartment." That hurt. But my kids were just being kids: open, innocent, unfiltered. Each of these comments was a celebration of good times and special moments we'd had together. I realized, after placing my ego aside, that the most helpful thing I could do was to join them in celebrating these memories. After all, they were *our* memories. The new chapter of your lives proceeds from the previous one, but it shouldn't supplant or erase it. Uphold and celebrate the previous stage while helping your kids transition to the new one.

––––––––––––

Part of demonstrating solidarity with your ex to your kids is resisting the urge to compete with her. Your kids benefit most when they feel close to, loved by, and securely attached to both of you. Your goal should be for them to get to a place where they feel equally safe, comfortable, and loved in both environments, and, most important, feel no need to take sides.

When the kids speak positively about their experiences with your ex, see this for the good thing it is. When they tell you how great the movie was she took them to, they're telling you because they want you to be part of their experience. You may feel jealous and have the instinct to take them to an even *better* movie, or maybe to criticize the one they saw with her, but if you really want to do right by them, try saying something like "That's great. I'm glad you guys had such a good time," or maybe "Cool. What was your favourite part?" Don't try to be the better parent; strive to be a great co-parent.

Your kids don't keep score. They love you because you protect and shelter them, challenge them to be their best, give them rules and structure, and shower them with affection. They don't love you because of your video game system, the restaurants you take them to, or the square footage of your home. There is no point in competing about anything versus your ex, because, even if you're keeping a tally, they aren't.

Just as you shouldn't compete about stuff, you also shouldn't compete about parenting styles. Psychotherapist Kyle Karalash puts it this way: "A common mistake parents tend to make is the discussing of parenting or relational concerns about the other. Children should not overhear your opinions about how the other person parents, nor complaints about differences between households."

Unfortunately, at certain moments, the thing that often makes kids so endearing — their complete lack of a filter — may also inadvertently stoke your competitive instinct. Let's say the kids are on a trip with your ex, and when you speak to them they tell you what an amazing time they're having. Don't let yourself go down the rabbit hole of imagining that she's "winning," or that you have to immediately start planning a vacation to equal or better hers. They are telling you because kids want to tell their parents stuff. Regardless of how old you are, when you accomplish something — at work, personally, in any context — who are the first people you want to tell? Your parents, right? And you're an alleged grown-up.

(As I write these words, it's Christmas and the kids are on a ski vacation with my ex. Dustin calls every day to tell me how awesome the conditions are, how great the place is, and how much fun they're having. At base level, this makes me jealous. But if I remove my ego, then I can hear myself saying the right words: *He's doing that to make you part of it, dumb-ass.*)

Let me repeat the point, since it's one I had a tough time accepting. Your kids never report positive experiences with your ex to make you feel jealous or inspire you to one-up. They do it because they're your kids and they want you to know what's going on in their lives. They do it because they miss you, and they want you to be part of the experience. They do it because they are too wonderfully guileless to ever imagine you'd be upset by what they say. Believe this. It will help you avoid a lot of unnecessary angst and be a better dad to your kids. I mean, do you want them to have a *bad* time when they go away with her?

The reverse of competition mentality is what I call positive-facilitation mentality. Instead of being competitive and possessive about your kids when it comes to your ex, encourage their relationship with her. There are many ways to do this. Omit clauses in your separation agreement that would prevent or minimize contact with her. When you're away with the kids, encourage them to check in with her. Speak positively about her in front of them. Offer to do things that are beyond the scope of your legal obligations — if she's coming back from a trip, for example, ask the kids if they'd like to surprise her with an airport pickup. Their reactions will make you want to do these kinds of things often, and they'll show you that it's possible to still feel like a family, just a differently configured one.

Want to know another great thing to do? Send your ex pictures of the kids when you're with them. Not just show-off pictures like when you're taking them somewhere great, but everyday pictures like doing homework, eating a meal, or goofing around. This, too, shows that you're not trying to shut out your ex, and that, even though you no longer live together under the same roof, you can still celebrate the miracle of your kids together.

One of the oddest things about a separation is the transition from co-parenting in the same space to co-parenting remotely — leading separate lives while being connected by the most constant and important thread of your life. You're now physically apart but still deeply entwined with your ex, and, as mentioned once or twice, the health of your kids depends more than anything else on the two of you being able to communicate well.

Most of the messages you exchange are going to happen not as live communication but as correspondence. When you lived together, of course, most of your communication happened face to face; now most of it is going to happen in written form. And you need to get good at it.

It's common for my ex and me to correspond a dozen times a day, via text, email, phone calls, or other means. We're better at communicating now than we were at first. These days, we do well when we're clear, direct, and succinct with each other, and when we maintain focus on the kids. We do less well when we cram multiple topics into the same communication, use multiple channels to communicate about the same topic, or, worst of all, let emotion take over, since once this happens, any hope of a mutually productive conversation is over.

I know I'm not the first person to tell you to stay cool when communicating with your ex. I'm going to say it anyway, because it's vital emotionally/internally (you will be constantly depleted if you let yourself function at a fever pitch of negative emotion all the time) and also practically/legally (everything you write down is potential evidence of something — like showing how angry you can get, if you're not careful).

Conversations will be hard for a while. One of the greatest difficulties I experienced in the first months after my split was the seeming inability to get two minutes into any dialogue with my ex without the conversation deteriorating into tension and frustration on one or both sides. There will no doubt be many times when you'll feel like exploding. Resist it. There will be times when you feel it's wrong to do anything but unload. Resist it. There will be times when you compose a text or email that you know is recklessly angry. Your thumb will be hovering over the button and you'll be just dying to click send. Resist it.

Here are some specific instances in which you may feel like giving your ex an earful:

- When you've had a bad day.
- When you feel like you've been calm for weeks and you feel you should be entitled to let loose already.
- When you start to think people telling you that being composed will serve you well in the long run is baloney and actually telling the truth would be best — or at least it would make you feel better.
- When you've stopped yourself from saying what's on your mind because your kids are around, and at this particular moment, they aren't around.

In all of these situations, you must — guess what I'm going to say? — resist it. Don't be aggressive. Don't be insulting. Don't be demeaning. Do not bait. Do not get baited. Do not pick fights. Do not retaliate. Do not write or say inflammatory things just because it feels better to do so.

Let's say you keep your cool for three months, but then one night you get so steamed that you allow yourself to get to that place where you're all like, "You want to do this? Let's *do this*!" and before you know it you've sent her a really mean and insulting text — just one. A year later, though you could not have foreseen it, you're in court fighting over custody. Your ex has never sent you any texts that could be considered aggressive or threatening. But there's that one you sent that shows that, well, maybe sometimes you snap. It might not count for anything in court. Or it might count for a lot. Get what I'm saying?

Listen to Yshai Boussi, who says, "Each parent may feel resentment and a wish to just get away from the other, but it's not that simple. When there isn't positive communication and planning between the parents, it's the kids who suffer. The amount of time it takes the family to make the transition to a new normal will depend largely on the parents' ability to resolve matters between them."

Understand and accept that the two of you are different people who have different styles of communicating, just as you did when you lived together. Try not to hold those differences against each other, and don't ask the other person to adopt your communication style. Instead, do your best to find a constructive joint approach. This includes reserving the mutual right to temporarily disengage. For example, a relatively common post-breakup syndrome is that one of the partners (most likely the person who decided to leave) becomes businesslike and focused on the practical needs of the split, while the other still wants to talk about feelings and emotions. It's perfectly fair for one of you to say, "I'm sorry, but we said we were going to talk about the contents of the house, and you seem to be more focused on other things, so I'd rather try again later." And it's also fine for the other person to say, "It's killing me that it seems so easy for you to talk about dividing up our things. I need to go, okay?" Allowing each other these temporary deferrals, as long as they don't go on indefinitely, is better than pursuing a conversation that has no chance of gaining traction.

There are two fundamental reasons why you need to get good at communicating with your ex. The first is to embed an ongoing positive dynamic. You have a simple choice: you're either going to build the habit of positive or negative communication, functional or dysfunctional, so the more you start to build the positives now, the better this will serve your kids. "The rule of thumb," says psychotherapist Dipti Shah, "is that if the parents can get along together, then the kids can be helped with this unexpected and significant event in their lives more quickly. It's a turning point that creates loss and turmoil inside them, requiring considerable internal and external resources to help overcome the change without any adverse effects to their other developmental processes. The key to this is good communication, so that both parents are appearing to sing from the same hymn sheet."

The second reason is a practical one: to facilitate the continuous back-and-forthing of stuff. The most difficult part of establishing a new normal, outside of the raw pain of not seeing your kids every day, is managing the ongoing transfer of things. There's a good chance the situation will feel a bit chaotic at first, since the fresher the split, the higher the emotions, therefore the harder it will be for you and your ex to work together calmly and reasonably. Plus, these circumstances are new to both of you, entailing a huge learning curve. The back and forth of the kids' stuff just happens to be the most prevalent aspect.

You'll likely forget stuff of theirs all the time at first. You may feel there's an imbalance, whereby kids think of one place as the real home, and therefore the permanent place for their stuff, and the other as a secondary place where they bring their stuff temporarily. This may especially hold for a certain period if one of you keeps the matrimonial home and the other moves somewhere new.

The back and forth was a huge drain on my family during the first three years after our split, primarily because I was living at my parents' place during that time, half an hour from the house. Dustin has had a mini-pillow (called Pillow) since he was very small. Cory has a sweet teddy bear (Bear) that he loves. Alisha has a soft pink blanket (Blankey), which she adores. Numerous times I would realize late in the evening that I still had Pillow, Bear, or Blankey with me from the night before and therefore had to get in the car and drive the hour (counting both ways) to return them — never mind the heartbreak of driving the half-hour only to leave Pillow, Bear, or Blankey in front of the house for my ex to pick up, or to execute a quick, quiet handover at the front door, knowing my kids were there inside.

Five years into our separation, I'd love to tell you that we have the system down. We've certainly become better at it, but I'm not sure it can ever be completely mastered, since there are always things that travel between places. Even if you're able to ensure a sufficient amount of the kids' stuff in both homes, there are still, for example, clothes, schoolbooks, and lunch thermoses that will sometimes leave one place in the morning and arrive at the other at the end of the day. (This is funny. I was working on the section above and then paused to grab something to eat. During my fifteen-minute break, I received a call from Cory asking if I could bring his boots to the house because he wants to play snow football with his friends, a text from my ex asking if I have Alisha's dress shoes because she needs them for a bat mitzvah this weekend, and an email from Dustin requesting I drop off his basketball sneakers on the way to work in the morning. I'm not making this up.)

On top of the daily back-and-forthing of your kids' stuff, there is the practical issue of decoupling the things you and your ex shared — big things like bank accounts, investments, credit cards, car leases, and mortgages, as well as items that may seem smaller but can be lightning rods, like bicycles, gardening tools, and luggage. The list is long, and you will need plenty of time, energy, and resources to get it all divided. In isolation, this division of property would be a simple enough exercise, but you're attempting to do it while also trying to do your job, stay healthy, get sleep, raise your kids, and remain mostly sane.

In other words, there's the need for productive *communication* between you and your ex, and there is the need for rock-solid *organization* between the two of you as well. I talked about communication already. Now let's deal with organization. Effectively managing the practical back and forth will contribute mightily to facilitating the overall psychological sea of change for you as a family. The less energy you need to use stressing about missing clothes and disorganized backpacks, the more mental and emotional resources you'll have to help your kids from one hour of their journey to the next (and this process really is hour to hour).

You'll see the results of this in action. When you and your ex are organized, you'll observe your kids being happier, calmer, and more themselves. On the flip side, moments that highlight kids living two different lives can intensify their internal chaos and anxiety. Such moments do not usually result from any emotional deficiency on your part, but of some absent practical need in a particular moment. School supplies are a common example. It is dreadful when you don't have the glue, stapler, ruler, paper, or pencil sharpener one of your kids needs to complete an assignment due tomorrow when those items are in full supply at their other home. The solution? Be an organizational machine. Find out from your kids what they need before they need it. Confirm with their teachers. Always have extras of the essentials on hand, and know where they are (as opposed to, "Markers? Sure — I think they're around here somewhere …"). There is no such thing as being too organized.

How do you get organized? Develop a system! Use tools! And templates! And charts and tables! Capture and organize all of the information relevant to your kids' lives and manage it closely, together with your ex. Many tools are available to help you achieve this, and there's no excuse for not doing it. Advises therapist Lindsey Jay Walsh, "I believe the most frequent issues dads going through a split encounter involve scheduling, and scheduling involves communication. It's usually difficult for people to maintain fruitful lines of communication with their exes. But you need to put in your best effort to do so."

Create a weekly shared to-do list to help divide tasks. Remove emotion from the powder keg of financial matters by maintaining a spreadsheet showing who has paid for what over which periods. Using such tools enhances clarity and transparency, reduces guessing or presumption, and, most important, makes co-management of your kids' lives as efficient and congruent as possible.

Think about their extracurricular activities. Using my own situation as an example, the kids do a variety of activities over the span of a week, including basketball, swimming, dance, rock climbing, and community programs. The logistics can be a major source of frustration between you and your ex if you aren't on top of them together. You can minimize family stress by planning well — who's going where, who's dropping off, who's picking up, who's organizing the carpool, who's responsible for packing the water bottle, whose job is it to make sure the right socks are available and not still in the washing machine.

This may all sound hyper-anal, but I can tell you that any split couple who have tried to co-manage their kids' lives the ad hoc way versus the proactive way will tell you that hyper-anal is far more preferable. In addition to developing and maintaining a mutual calendar for your kids' activities, I also suggest creating a shared file containing all relevant information about their critical documents: passports, birth certificates, social security numbers, immunization records, and anything else that might need to be produced quickly. Determine who is responsible for keeping the physical versions of each document, and always share with the other parent as soon as any gets updated.

Your number one goal is to minimize tension for your kids. Being organized reduces stress on them by reducing stress on you and your ex. Furthermore, because the two of you are going to have to pass through an unavoidable period of heightened emotion, you may experience, during difficult moments, both a lower level of tolerance as well as, again, a quicker impulse to want to blame the other person when stuff goes wrong. The more organized you are, the more you reduce the chances of stuff going wrong — not getting the forms in on time for a school field trip, say, or one of you taking the kids out of town only to arrive at the airport and realize one of their passports has expired. (I've witnessed this more than once.)

With a little organization, which doesn't take much effort but does require good communication (there it is again!), you can do a lot to minimize potential disruptions. Your kids being able to hear even one conversation in which one of you says, "Do you happen to have the kids' passport numbers handy?" and the other replies, "Sure, I'll send them to you right now" can do wonders for the way they feel inside. Think of every moment as one that can either increase your kids' sense of calm and reassurance or compound their feelings of distress and fear. Communicating in a positive mode with your ex, and being organized in a unified way, helps you accomplish the one goal that really matters: smoothing your kids' individual transitions, and your collective passage as a family, to a happier and more harmonious place.

Ten Questions: My Buddy Marcello

What were the biggest mistakes you made with your kids during your split, and how have you addressed them?
Although I'm guilty of not being a perfect father, I have tried my best to minimize the impact of the split on my daughter. I would say I was sometimes guilty of putting her on the spot — asking her, for instance, to make a decision on something my ex and I couldn't agree on. It's never fair to put one's kids in the middle. It puts them in an impossible position since they don't want to upset either parent. They shouldn't be part of the drama.

Also, on occasion, I've made tongue-in-cheek remarks about my ex within earshot of my daughter. I knew this was wrong, but frustration sometimes got the best of me. I realized this was wrong and corrected it.

The important thing during a split is to stay present to what's happening and adjust your approach. This introspection should be done on a day-to-day basis and adjusted through your children's different ages and stages, since their reactions will go through various cycles.

What's been your greatest challenge?
Protecting access to my daughter. Fourteen years after our split, my ex continues to try to sabotage it. She intentionally plans fun things during my days or weekends that are difficult for my daughter to pass up. I recently lost my every-other-weekend rotation and now only see her every three weeks. I also lost every other Monday a few years ago because my ex decided to schedule a recurring after-school activity that day of the week.

Another challenge was when my daughter didn't have email or a phone, and so I had no choice but to communicate with her through my ex. I would leave messages that she often said she never received, and my ex would screen my calls so I would only get her voice mail.

Can you describe your lowest or hardest moments with your kids?
There was a period of almost three months where I didn't speak to my daughter. This was my lowest point since the actual breakup. My legal bills were through the roof and I was living in a basement apartment. My daughter, eleven at the time, was cancelling plans with me and not returning my calls. The problem escalated as time went on, and I grew angrier. The last straw occurred when she wanted to cancel yet another weekend with me for no discernible reason. I finally emailed her a long message saying she was being selfish. She had all of us who loved her and wanted to see her and was casting us aside. I told her we were not a hotel she could check in and out of, and that her behaviour was not only confusing to us adults but to her two- and four-year-old sisters, who didn't know why they weren't seeing her. I gave her an ultimatum that she either smarten up or not come over anymore. I waited for her call, which never came. I desperately wanted her to miss us and eventually call, but my bluff didn't work. Eventually we cleared the air and got back on a good path. Some would see this as a parenting error (I did for

a long time), but I believe this break was needed for her to appreciate what her dad (and his side) had to offer, and our importance in her life.

How about moments when you saw light at the end of the tunnel?
There were many moments that indicated things were getting better. Some were insignificant, others big. I would say the biggest was when my daughter was able to start talking and communicating with me, since she'd been only eight months old at the time of our split. When I was able to start talking to her about things, I was able to tweak my parenting approach accordingly. A big event was when I started seriously dating my now wife, and our eventually marrying. The key is to keep thinking positively and being the best dad you can be. I kept reminding myself that I didn't fail; my marriage did. As I started to slowly rebuild my life with my new wife and the kids we then had, as well as my financial situation, all while improving my relationship with my daughter, everything started to make sense again. Also, the loving, harmonious nature of my new marriage built my confidence, reminding me again that I am a good husband and father. When my new wife and I had disagreements, we handled them with mutual trust and respect. This wasn't the case with my ex. We were like fire and gas.

In your view, what do kids need most from their dad during or after a breakup?
Kids need to feel safe and secure while their parents are separating. This should be a shared responsibility, but one can only control their own behaviour. I learned that all I could do was to be as present and supportive as possible. Although I must admit I pretty much despise my ex, I made sure to continually turn the other cheek and try to get along with her as best as I could. I made many concessions to avoid conflict, often at the expense of my happiness or financial solidity. Early in our split, I took an early child education course, and later, another called the Landmark Forum to help me with overall parenting, conflict resolution, and creating breakthroughs.

Another important thing is to establish a routine. Once my access schedule was established (through our lawyers), I stuck by it like glue, never missing anything.

How much emotion did you show your kids with regard to your split? Where do you stand on how much "real" they should see versus how much they should be protected?

You need to manage your emotions around your kids. I'm not saying be a robot, I'm just saying that if you're not careful and you allow yourself to show too much, you can cause serious psychological trauma. I think it's fair to sometimes let emotion out to make a point, but overall it's your responsibility as a parent to stay balanced as an example to your kids. This goes back to what I was saying about making them feel stable and safe. If they have a crazy parent who yells and throws stuff across the room, or one that sobs and complains about everything, it will make them feel insecure, and likely withdraw.

What would you say are the key hurdles to get over as a family before kids can start adjusting to the new normal?

I was fortunate that my daughter was younger, but the key was establishing a healthy schedule and sticking to it. I know of other parents who split and then make up the schedule as they go, which I believe is really bad. A schedule avoids arguments and establishes a routine the children can not only adjust to, but also anticipate. Plus it's far easier for the parents to plan when they know the schedule.

How do you handle the practical issues of two households?

Early on, I had to come to terms with the fact that a fifty-fifty situation wouldn't work, nor would it be legally smart of me to challenge my ex on it. Courts only agree to this arrangement if both parents are amicable, which we were not. I anticipated arguments from the outset and made concessions to avoid them. I did this by agreeing to do all the pickups and drop-offs. It was a big commitment, but worth it because it meant I didn't have to coordinate with my ex.

Second, I made sure to create a true home environment for my daughter, with her own room, clothes, and belongings. Everything she needed was provided for, and as she grew, I replenished it all. She had her own bike, scooter, sports equipment, and so on.

Finally, my ex and I established a schedule that wouldn't interfere with the kids' sleep and school. For example, I would pick up my daughter straight from school on the Friday of my weekends with her, then drop her back on Sunday before dinner so that she could have dinner with her mom and still be in bed at a reasonable time to start the week.

What are your top three pieces of advice to other dads for maintaining a loving and healthy relationship with their kids after a split?
One, don't give up. You owe it to your kids to be there for them through thick and thin. Remember that they are new to this, on top of the normal trials of growing up, so be patient and loving.

Two, don't let your ex get to you. Remember that you split up for a reason. She is not going to magically become a different person. Look after yourself and your own affairs. Also, it's important to stay in shape so you can cope physically and mentally. Stress is a silent killer.

Three, don't give up on your dream of being with the right person. I almost gave up on it, but instead I ended up falling in love, and it's been amazing.

5

Negotiating Your Rights

B esides the emotional crucible you're in, you are also suddenly having to deal with a gajillion practical questions. It would be nice if
separations were simple or quick, but in the majority of cases, they
are neither. You and your ex share money, property, passwords, loyalty
points, flatware, and tons of miscellaneous stuff you didn't even think
about until the time arrived to divide it. Now you must figure out how
to disentangle all that, and the process is a gigantic pain in the posterior.
This chapter deals with the practical aspects of splitting up — no, it isn't
fun to discuss; yes, it is necessary to do so — starting with the most
common question split dads ask.

Do I need a lawyer?

This one gets a big "It depends" from me, with a side of "Every situation
is different." Let me start by saying that lawyers make money by practis-
ing law. My aim is not to throw lawyers under the bus. But I do want to
speak frankly. And here's how I think about lawyers. When I had rotator
cuff issues some years ago and told my doctor friend Ira that I'd been to a
surgeon for advice on whether I should get it operated on and the surgeon
said yes, Ira's advice was, "I'm not going to tell you what to do, but I will
say that surgeons like to do surgery."

There are many competent family and divorce lawyers, many of whom are lovely people. However, they, like you, need to feed their families. So the more complicated or drawn-out your case, the better for them. I dealt with a few different lawyers during my separation, and I will say candidly that they all drove me nuts. Here's why:

- They spoke too slowly. (If I wanted you to talk to me like I'm six, I would say, "Please talk to me like I'm six." Otherwise, please talk to me like a grown-up, and if there is something I don't understand, I will say, "I don't understand.")
- They said everything three times instead of once. (I write for a living. If I'm not clear and concise, I lose clients. I should be able to hold others to the same standard.)
- Their emails and letters were far more complicated than necessary. (I couldn't get over the feeling that they wrote in this manner knowingly.)
- They took too long to reply to my questions. (I know I'm not your only client, but if I'm paying you an arm and a leg per hour, please get back to me promptly.)
- When they did reply, they answered my simple questions with long, convoluted responses. (See point number 2.)
- Even the cheaper ones charged ludicrous fees. (No further comment on this, other than: Give me a break.)

In the ideal world, you and your ex would work things out amicably, or at least at a level of co-functionality that would make it unnecessary to pay lawyers to help. If the two of you can work together to agree on the three components that a separation agreement needs to contain — division of assets, custody schedule, and child and/or spousal support payments — then there is no reason you need to spend a nickel on lawyers.

Most split couples, of course, are not able to resolve things on their own. In many of these cases, however, I'm not sure the reasons for their using lawyers are good ones. I feel many couples could save a lot of money, time, and headaches by exercising a bit of patience, communicating better, and being more flexible. Here are the most common reasons I believe people turn to lawyers during a split.

- **They think they're supposed to.** You'll hear many people toss numbers at you — "You're going to spend twenty grand before you blink," or "You can expect to spend ten to fifteen large on a separation, but it's worth it." You come to believe that your first order of business should be to get a lawyer, when in fact your first act should be to step back, breathe, and see if you and your ex can engage in a civil discussion about where to go from here.

- **They listen to everyone around them.** In the midst of a breakup, you're in a fragile and impressionable state. People may give you guidance you feel is uncharacteristically aggressive or myopic — your parents because they love you, your divorced friends because they may have lingering hostility from their own splits, your lawyer friends because they believe nothing should be handled without the representation of those in the legal profession. Try not to be swayed. Do research, ask questions, learn from friends who have experienced divorce. And trust your own gut.

- **They're nervous about doing it on their own.** Yes, there are parts of the law that are esoteric. Yes, family law can be complicated. But we live in the information age. You can become conversant in nearly anything with a relatively small amount of research, including asking questions of those qualified to answer — those in the profession, or those who have gone through a split themselves. People often use lawyers because they fear that if they choose to handle any part of their breakup on their own, they may make a costly error. Again, the key factor here is the dynamic with your ex. Both of you lawyering up is like sending a mutual signal that you're steeling for battle. Try to replace an opening salvo with an olive branch. I know it may be easier said than done, but you have nothing to lose.

- **They do it out of anger.** At the beginning, and for a while after, everything that happens between you and your ex will occur at a peak of emotionality. In the best cases, this period is short, settling then into a more rational phase in which the two of you can start to have conversations without one or both of you flying off the handle. You may find it extremely difficult to separate the emotions you feel from the practical matters you need to resolve, but the more you can do so, the better off you, and your bank accounts, will be. Feel what you feel in your heart, but with regard to the practical parts of separating, use your head.

A separation does not have to be rocket science. Lawyers end up being used when people are too emotional, too nervous, too suggestible, or too intimidated to handle things on their own. But you can deal with issues on your own, probably more easily than you think. Doing so requires a bit of math, a lot of patience and flexibility, and, way up at the top of the list, the ability to put aside the laser-hot emotions of the situation in the interests of moving forward as a family.

What about mediators? Are they any better?

Here's the typical pattern. Couple breaks up. Both are upset, confused, and frightened. Couple knows they have to divide stuff, determine custody, and figure out who should pay what to whom. Couple tries to discuss these matters but realizes every conversation is at best a false start, at worst a stack of dynamite. Both of them ask friends and family about lawyers. When they see the rates, both try again to handle things by themselves, only to realize again that talking to each other is like trying to swim through a school of jellyfish on steroids. Couple hears from others that if they don't wish to pay lawyers' fees, they could use an alternative, mediators. They basically do the same job as lawyers, except in this case it's one person trying to facilitate the couple talking to each other instead of two people representing the two individuals in a war that they (the lawyers, not the couple) hope drags on indefinitely. In other words, mediators are cheaper, gentler versions of lawyers, and their job is to guide you through a conversation you haven't been able to manage on your own. They represent your kids as opposed to either of you, insofar as their role is to try to bring you to a fair middle ground on every element of the separation.

I'm afraid my view of mediators isn't much kinder than my view of lawyers. Sure, it's easier to have a third party act as a buffer between you two when you're really mad, but do you honestly want to pay someone to hold your hands through a hard conversation? Wouldn't it be better to have that hard conversation without throwing money out the window?

That all sounds great in theory, but you don't understand what I'm dealing with. She's impossible. What do I do?

How much or how little money you spend, either on lawyers or a mediator, depends almost entirely on how well or how poorly you are able to have conversations that don't spiral out of control. My ex and I went through what I would characterize as three stages after we decided to split. The first, in which just about any conversation between us was impossible, lasted about eighteen months. I call it *the wringer*. The emotions were too fresh, and there was too much bitterness. We pledged over and over to try to figure things out between us, since we both understood the simple equation of not wanting to spend money on lawyers that we could spend on our kids instead. But every time we tried, the conversations were laughably brief. Often after less than a minute, some invisible wire would be tripped. So we each hired a lawyer, even though we agreed we didn't want to.

The second stage, which lasted about another year, was one I'd call the stage of *guarded optimism*, since it entailed us kind-of-sort-of starting to be able to have sporadic dialogue that one might call constructive. At this point we were able to go a couple of minutes without one or both of us going off the deep end. In this way we could slowly start to discuss the items in the separation agreement in a manner that indicated we might perhaps, if the planets lined up properly, be able to get to the finish line of the process without spending oodles of money on lawyers. At the same time, we started to believe in each other's genuine intention to resolve matters fairly and amicably. We were able to leave aside thoughts of the other wanting to get revenge, act sneaky or manipulative, or continue to be so blind with anger that they would rather spend a ton on lawyers and hurt the other person than try to have a courteous and reasonable negotiation.

The third stage is one I'd term *escape velocity*, meaning we have finally come to a place where we're able to leave behind a lot of the previous ballast, and, even though many of the same resentments still exist, are generally able to let more mature traits shine through. The dynamic is still tenuous on many days, and we still argue about plenty of stuff, but disagreements happen less often than they did before, and with less likelihood of escalation. I have no idea how we compare to other split couples. All I can say is that I feel we've both tried our best to move forward while dealing with a constantly shifting kaleidoscope of difficult and complex emotions.

Why does it take so many couples, just as it took us, such a significant length of time to get to this point of relative semi-functionality? Lots of reasons.

- **Rarely do both members of a former couple go at the same pace.** If one of you left the other, you'll likely remain divergent in terms of how fast or slow you're inclined to decouple. The person who left, once having made the decision, may want to accelerate, while the other may want to slow down. One of you may be resentful of the other for being so calm, while the other may be upset that the first is so emotional. For a long while, my ex and I were so far from marching to the same drummer, we might as well have been in different bands.

- **Money is a hot-button issue.** One of you may be confident with finances, while the other may consider spreadsheets akin to Sanskrit. There's a reason money is the number one cause of fights among married couples. And if it causes problems with people who are together, well, with those who have split up, lord have mercy. Often the person more comfortable with numbers will find it easy to work out finances without the need for professional help, while the other person may not want to trust anyone but accountants and lawyers. My ex and I had this discrepancy in our views, which led to plenty of stops and starts, though eventually we got to where we needed to go. The process just took — sorry — time.

- **You're different people.** Even if the breakup was mutual, you're still two different individuals who operate in different ways. One of you may think lawyers or mediators are a waste, while the other may feel they're helpful. One of you may be highly organized, the other more scattered. One may travel frequently for work (or be looking for work), while the other has a steady and unchanging schedule. All this contributes to how fast you're able to move forward together in moving apart.

- **You're both wound up.** Understand that your attempts to "sit down and talk" will likely involve several derailments, especially in those first weeks and months when emotions are high. As mentioned, during that first stage, my ex and I tried multiple sit-downs, but inevitably, less than five minutes after sitting down, one of us had stormed out. Everything seemed to be a trigger. Phone calls, texts, and emails were no better — for months, we had almost no ability to sustain any kind of dialogue. Internal turmoil manifested in extreme external dysfunction. As former United States secretary of state Dean Acheson said, "Negotiating in the classic diplomatic sense assumes parties more anxious to agree than to disagree." We were not yet ready for diplomacy. We were still stuck.

So to answer your question (*She's impossible. What do I do?*), you try your best. If dialogue doesn't work the first time and you're able to give the issue at hand time to settle, you do that. Then you try again. You have to decide what's best and workable for your particular situation. Remember the spectrum: eventually things will move from left to right, though they likely won't move as fast or as smoothly as you wish they would.

As I said, my ex and I have managed, over the course of what feels like a long time but maybe in relative terms is not, to start talking more effectively and more peacefully. Calm, mutually respectful communication is still often hard, but not as hard as it was in those first couple of stages, when I often assumed we would never be able to reach a place of mutual civility. We did. You will too.

Okay, say we get to a point where we can try to do this without lawyers or mediators. I'm not a professional negotiator. How do I reach a deal that's fair? How will I even know if it's fair?

First, don't worry about your non-professional status. All you need is common sense, the ability to place emotion aside, and an understanding of the two essential parts of the definition of the word *negotiation*: a discussion aimed at reaching an agreement.

The first essential part is the word *discussion* — that is, one of you talks while the other listens, then the other talks while the first listens. You need to try to be active in your listening, and you need to make a superhuman effort not to interrupt or undermine each other. And, to the best of your ability, give each other the benefit of the doubt that what the other person is saying is being said from a place of sincerity and with reason and thought involved.

The second essential part is the word *agreement*. Not lopsided victory, Pearl Harbor job, clever end-around, bait and switch, or steal of the century, but agreement — in other words, a conclusion in which both people reach a point of satisfaction. A *discussion*, to reach an *agreement*. Note that the definition of negotiation is not "A situation in which two people yell at each other while frequently ignoring everything the other says until both people throw their arms up in exasperation."

Here are five principles that are key to a productive and successful negotiation between exes, in which hopefully no one gets murdered. Sorry, did I say that out loud?

- **Give every decision proper time and consideration.**
  One of the reasons it takes so much time to get from the

beginning to the "end" of a separation is that, even if your life is modest, the two of you still have a bewildering amount of stuff to discuss and divide. You have the task of taking everything contained in what was a shared life and organizing it into two.

Notice I say "organizing" instead of separating, because, even though your lives are going to become separate in many ways, they are at the same time going to remain intertwined. It's not a simple exercise of moving this into column A and that into column B. My ex and I didn't own much, yet at times, things still felt overwhelmingly complicated. (Where do we keep the bikes? How about the framed pictures of the kids? Who gets the gardening tools? How about that nice vase we got as a wedding gift, or the spice rack, or the living-room rug, or the painting we bought at that auction? What about all the coffee-table books? Who gets the printer?)

I never felt like we had a lot of stuff until we had to divide it. And doing that can get so complicated, exhausting, and sad that you may succumb to either of two common judgment errors. One is asking for too much; the other is asking for too little. Both these things happen when emotions take over. Try not to let them.

- **Have a plan.** Know your must-haves, nice-to-haves, and don't-really-cares. Or, as my friend Greg puts it, "Take a firm stance on certain subjects and do not compromise on things that you feel you should not. Compromise on things that you won't regret." You want it to be a kind negotiation, but it is a negotiation, so prepare as much as you can to try to produce as successful an outcome as you can. As Henry Kissinger said, "If you do not know where you are going, every road will get you nowhere."

- **Give yourself an emotion-ectomy before you start.** When negotiating, try your best not to make decisions in the heat of the moment. The more reasonable and equitable resolution you can strike, the better it will be for your kids, and the more integrity you both will feel in retrospect. Your kids will benefit if you negotiate in a fair but firm way. They will not benefit if you fight tooth and nail for every dinner plate and coaster, or, by the same token, if you hand over the farm simply because you're exhausted from so much negotiating. There may be moments when all the debating, fighting, and arguing tempts you to say "Fine, whatever, I just don't want to argue anymore." Take time to pause, breathe, and continue. Negotiation is a tiring process, but one you need to see through.

- **Remember the definition of negotiation:** *a discussion to reach an agreement.* That means it's about two people ending up satisfied enough. Don't go into it trying to win; go into it trying to resolve. Your goal is to arrive at the best situation, for you, your ex, and your kids. Yes, your ex is included in this threefold goal, because she will need to provide for them the same way you will. This may sound strange, but one way to conduct an effective negotiation is to start not by asking what a good resolution would look like for you, but what it would look like for her. As author and business psychologist Harvey Robbins says, "Place a higher priority on discovering what a win looks like for the other person." If one of you tries to bleed the other dry or come away with a disproportionate amount of things or rights, it's your kids who will get the short end of the stick. You are not trying to defeat or take down your ex. You are trying to arrive at a resolution that will allow your kids to have two loving homes, two caring and present parents, and the smoothest possible transition to your new chapter as a family. Here's some wise advice from Karl Albrecht, a German entrepreneur who started a discount supermarket chain with his brother and became one of the wealthiest people in the world: "Start out with an ideal and end up with a deal."

- **Recognize that you can be a fair negotiator without having to turn into an aggressive jerk.** People may tell you that you're too nice. Ignore them. They may offer you advice that you know is skewed by their own biases. Ignore that too. They may tell you your situation is exactly like the one their friend went through. It isn't. Remain yourself. Remain neutral. Maintain focus and practise restraint. Remain objective, to every extent possible. Remain calm. And stay focused on the kids.

As I've said a few times now, if you and your ex act reasonably with each other, you have a decent chance of being able to get a separation agreement done without needlessly involving lawyers and draining your wallet. Here are my top ten pieces of advice for drafting a separation agreement:

1. **Ask friends who have gone through divorce if they would share a copy of their agreement with you.** They'll probably be more than happy to. Several of my friends shared theirs with me, which I used to cobble together my own draft. Or just use one of the many free online templates, which are all pretty much the same.

2. **Do some homework.** Understand what specific elements are required in a separation agreement in your region, province, state, or country. The requirements vary in different jurisdictions.

3. **Make the language as simple and straightforward as possible.** Do not use complex sentence structure or fancy words. Make it concise. In short, write it opposite to the way a lawyer would.

4. **Draft it with both you and your ex in mind.** See my comments earlier in this chapter. Try not to draft a document that transparently has you "winning" the separation, since that will only offend your ex and lead to a longer and more hostile negotiation. Come up with a draft that you feel is as fair as possible on both sides, which will start you off closer

to the end. Heed the words of eighteenth-century politician Henry Boyle: "The most important trip you can make is meeting someone halfway."

5. **Err on the side of specificity.** The separation agreement you ultimately file with the courts is meant to act as a legal guide and reference document. So make it exact, even where you think it may not need to be. For example, one mistake I made was agreeing to the general clause that my ex and I would "divide all contents of the matrimonial household." I was confident we'd be able to do it ourselves, plus I couldn't stomach the idea of going through everything in the house to decide what would go to whom. We came close. But a few years later we're still arguing over one or two valuable items, which is a bummer. Be as precise as you can about as much as you can.

6. **Don't try to be clever.** People will give you lots of armchair advice about negotiating. They'll tell you to ask for more than you really want, to leave room for negotiation downward. They'll tell you to be aggressive, to make a statement that you're not to be messed with. They'll tell you to use lots of blustery language, to put your ex on her heels. They'll tell you to hire a ruthless legal shark. Lots of people told me to do lots of this stuff. I ignored them all. Your best negotiation tactic is to be open and calm in the spirit of resolving things as quickly and smoothly as possible. You're trying to come up with a document that will enable you, your ex, and your kids to move on in a fair and practicable way.

7. **When you send the draft separation agreement to your ex, be an open book about the process you used.** Here's what I wrote to my ex: "I wanted to take a shot at drafting an agreement, since every dollar we spend on lawyers is money that doesn't go to the kids. Some friends shared their agreements with me, and I used different parts of those, combined with a bunch of research, to create this. Could you review it and let me know what you think? My

understanding is that we're allowed to draft this ourselves, and all we need to pay a lawyer for is filing it with the courts." Take any mystery and suspicion out of it. A little good faith can go a long way.

8. **Know the legal process.** Once the two of you have agreed to the contents of the agreement (fingers crossed!), call your municipal family court and ask what the requirements are in terms of filing. Here in Ontario, for example, both parties need to formally acknowledge whether they have consulted a lawyer as part of the process.

9. **Get free advice.** If you have any lawyer friends, ask if they'd be willing to have a look at your draft and tell you whether they think it would stand up in court. They probably will, and it probably would.

10. **Include the proper caveats.** Where relevant, indicate that certain clauses may be subject to change, and under what circumstances. For example, maybe your ex is a teacher and gets summers off, so you agree to give her more time with the kids during that period. Be sure to include language such as "while both parties remain in their current jobs," or something to that effect, so that if things change, you aren't tied to the agreement.

I said at the beginning of this chapter that the most common question asked by separated dads is "Do I need a lawyer?" The second most common question: "Is the system really biased against dads?" Well, yeah, kind of. It seems a bit ridiculous to many of us modern dads who are just as involved in the lives of our kids as moms, but understand that most of today's legal rules are holdovers from a time when fathers' roles were very different. It wasn't that long ago that almost all men worked, almost all women stayed home, and the average dad was, to put it kindly, not exactly the model of an involved co-parent. The laws written to reflect the needs of the men and women of that period remain, to a significant degree, in effect today — a situation that often puts dads behind the eight ball. The system has started to catch up, but not much. Here's a cautionary tale I heard from one of the dads I spoke to:

Back in the eighties, it was still fairly automatic that the mother got custody. This was the case for me. Then, after five years of separation, my children came to live with me. At about age fourteen, my daughter became displeased with my wanting to know where she went, with whom, and when, so she called her mom, who asked to meet with me only to say that there was no way either Jennifer or Michael could come back with her, explaining that it was best they stay with me to finish high school.

When I came home from work the next day, my son was sitting at the kitchen table. He said, "You're not going to be happy." I went upstairs to find Jennifer's room empty. Her mom had changed her mind, taken her out of school that morning, packed her clothes from my place, and vanished. When I pressed the school and the court, they said I didn't have custody, so there was nothing they could do about it. Fight for your say. Always.

That happened a while ago, but as I said, a lot of inherent bias still remains within the system, so I want you to be aware of the playing field and be able to play effectively on it. Let's talk about your rights as a dad and what you can do to ensure they're properly granted.

My first piece of advice: don't accept any of the system's built-in assumptions. For example, don't accept that dads should only be allowed "visitation" or "access" while moms are granted the right of primary care, or that the default when a couple splits is that Mom stays in the matrimonial home and Dad gets a new place. This may well be the scenario that makes the most sense in your situation, but it ought not to be assumed. As psychotherapist Kyle Karalash says,

> A common notion I hear from split fathers is that they're expected to become absent. There seems to be a social stigma that assumes that when parents separate, it is the father's fault, and/or he will take off and leave the mother

to be sole caretaker. They seem to have to fight against this idea that they are unfit, uncaring, or emotionally incapable. I have worked with several men who want to explore their identity as a single dad and prove that they can be, or already are, just as involved in the lives of their children as Mom.

It's important to assert clearly that you are as equal a presence in your kids' lives as your ex. For this reason, I made sure to strike out words such as *visitation, access,* and *non-custodial* right from the start of my negotiation process. You are not a person who visits your kids, and you don't need to be given "access" to them. You are their father, and you and their mom have split up. In my view, it's bad for the kids if either parent is given the legal status of a visitor or someone with "access." It makes you sound like a criminal on parole. I already felt miserable enough having to drop off my kids to my ex on certain nights; I sure as heck wasn't going to be described as a visitor, and I wasn't going to accept any kind of default position that resulted in the kids staying with me Wednesdays and every other weekend. These kinds of assumptions are, as I said, relics from a time when it made sense for moms to be seen as the default primary caregivers. I love being a dad more than anything, and I'm proud of how involved I am in my kids' lives. I'm sure you are too. Demand that this involvement be recognized, no matter what archaic legal guidelines might say.

With that in mind, I want to say something, and I want to try to say it with both sensitivity and directness. I hope your situation proceeds smoothly. I hope you and your ex can get along. I hope there are no bumps along the way. However, people don't always play nice during a split. Emotions get crazy, reason can go out the window, and a lot of our less-than-impressive traits can take over. So you need to be smart. Not devious or manipulative, just smart. Document everything. Save every email. Take a screenshot of all text messages. When making arguments or composing responses, write from a place of facts and logic, not emotions. I don't want you to be cynical or jaded; I just want you to cover your bases. I'm not encouraging you to have a negative attitude or assume that everything is going to go badly. I just want you to make sure you're covered.

As with every other part of the process, I encourage you to be open, calm, and as collaborative as possible. When it comes to calculating support, for example, the formulas are pretty straightforward — the main inputs are your respective incomes, the number of kids you have, and where you live. The formulas may be easy but, of course, that doesn't mean that coming to an agreement will be simple. I won't be naive and tell you that couples don't often fight about who is entitled to what, but again, it's easier if you can keep the negotiation between the two of you and away from lawyers. Once they get involved, you will immediately start doing things like exchanging full financial disclosures, income statements, and tax returns, and the amount of paperwork and administration will be exhausting. Equalizing finances is something you can do yourself using fairly simple online calculators.

The same goes for dividing expenses. Talk about costs in detail with your ex, and make them as specific and prescriptive as possible so that the two of you do not have to spend time later arguing over or interpreting what you've agreed to. One method is to divide all major child expenses fifty-fifty and agree that everything else is paid by the parent who has the kids at a given time. In my case, for example, major expenses are school tuition, registration fees for sports, music lessons and other programs, and overnight camp. My ex and I split those down the middle, and all other expenses were agreed to be the responsibility of the custodial parent at any given time.

Alternatively, you can try to reconcile all expenses at even intervals: say, getting together every quarter to show each other all expenses paid by each of you during that period (with receipts) and then doing a simple reconciliation — whoever paid more in that period gets reimbursed by the other for half the difference. Again, always demonstrate that your goal is to co-operate and to be an effective co-parent. Show that you're not trying to hide anything or be cunning or unscrupulous.

Recently I paid a lot of money to replace some of the kids' ski equipment. These weren't part of our agreed major expenses, so I wasn't entitled to request reimbursement from my ex, but I still felt like I'd laid out a lot of dough. I could have written her something like "I just paid a bundle for the kids' ski gear. I know it isn't part of the agreement, but you should pay me back for half." Here's what I wrote instead:

> I was thinking that, regarding one-off stuff we pay for, maybe it would make sense to agree on a minimum threshold for which the other is responsible for reimbursing half, like two hundred dollars or something. E.g., if one of us buys something for one of the kids that's seventy-five dollars, there's no reimbursement required, but for anything exceeding two hundred dollars, we reimburse for half the cost. I'm sure sometimes you feel like you're spending more than I am, and I sometimes feel that way too, but the truth is we both spend a ton on them all the time, and this would be a way for us both to feel like there's a control in place to keep it balanced. For example, I just spent a lot of money on all the ski stuff, but I know you have an equal number of those situations, too, and I don't want either of us to feel like we're spending disproportionately to the other. My idea is that we keep any receipts over the agreed threshold and then reconcile at the end of each month. What do you think? And if you agree, what do you think is a reasonable threshold?

This email was my way of trying to begin the conversation positively. I urge you to try to do the same as often as you can. That doesn't mean your talks about finances or other sensitive practical matters will all go well. Often they won't. But you can always start out calm and kind, and adjust your approach when needed. Be objective. Be transparent. Be as fair as you can. But fight for your rights as a dad. You deserve them.

———————

Ten Questions: My Friend Shel

What were the biggest mistakes you made with your kids during your split, and how have you addressed them?
If I made any mistakes, they were likely pre-marriage, when I signed off on prenups that didn't properly contemplate life with kids. When you end up in a world where one side has or makes much more than the other — which is my situation — it's hard to balance lifestyles. So trying to be a good sport and not caring about money might have been a mistake. Sometimes having a fight is in the best interests of the kids. You can't sacrifice your position every time there is a disagreement because you "don't want to fight and upset the kids." Sometimes you know better, and need to stick to your guns.

What's been your greatest challenge?
Diverging financial positions. For example, right now my kids are on a three-week trip to Asia with my ex. Since I can't afford that kind of trip, I technically lose time with my kids by allowing them to have this experience.

Can you describe your lowest or hardest moments with your kids?
Maybe the "I'm moving to Mom's or Dad's house because you're making me" experience. Both my ex and I refuse to entertain such comments, so that helps, but there are moments when I do worry my kids will find my house too strict and want to go live with her exclusively, since they'll have a bigger room, better gaming system, pool, and lots of other stuff I can't give them.

How about moments when you saw light at the end of the tunnel?
Finding a new partner was big. I felt a lightening.

In your view, what do kids need most from their dad during or after a breakup?
Stability. Strength. Time.

How much emotion did you show your kids with regard to your split? Where do you stand on how much "real" they should see versus how much they should be protected?

I don't talk about the cause of our divorce or share those kinds of details with them. If they ask, I just say things weren't working out. When they're older, they'll likely figure it out. I don't care what they know; I just want them to be happy. I try to limit displays of anger in front of them. It's never good for kids to see that conflict.

What would you say are the key hurdles to get over as a family before kids can start adjusting to the new normal?

My kids seemed to handle the split easily, but they were young. Having a new, fun place for them is key. Being around is key. There was no custody scenario less than fifty-fifty that I was willing to accept, and I think my kids benefit from having equal time with both parents.

How do you handle the practical issues of two households?

My ex and I live close, so as much as we fight about who forgot this or that, we try hard not to make the kids feel bad when something is left behind. Our agreed position is, "It's your stuff, be responsible for it," but also, "We'll help you if you forget, and won't get mad." Checklists help.

What are your top three pieces of advice to other dads for maintaining a loving and healthy relationship with their kids after a split?

One, be present. Use your time with them well. Two, try to have an economic balance between the two homes. Three, frame everything from a "kids first" perspective and you can't go wrong.

6

Ensuring Your Safety

Nothing prepared you for a marital breakup. Maybe you were the one who finally left after considering it for a while. Maybe you got blindsided. Maybe the relationship simply passed the point of no return and, despite attempts to resuscitate it, at some point you and your partner just knew it was over. Regardless of the circumstances leading to your split, you are now thrust into the reality of living in the aftermath, and baby, it's hard. As American author Rick Yancey puts it in his novel *The Last Star*, "You're never perfectly safe. No human being on Earth ever is or ever was. To live is to risk your life, your heart, everything."

Even if you've been pretty much the steady, responsible type till now — maybe especially if you've been that type — you might be feeling so much pressure that you find yourself wanting to let loose. Maybe you want to get a little wild, or a lot wild, as a way of rebelling against how generally awful you feel. You might be such a powder keg of tension that you're looking for some way to unleash, and the weekly game of pickup with your buddies isn't doing the job. You might feel like you want to give the world the finger by acting stupid, even if you know it isn't smart or reasonable. Maybe *because* it isn't.

That's fine — but no matter how stressed you're feeling, or how angry, or sad, or desperate you are, you're a father whose children need you. This means you need to make sure you don't do something you might permanently regret, or which might unfairly impact others or, worse, compromise your relationship with your children. There can be a fine line between letting loose a little and acting truly reckless, and the way you feel right now has the potential to blind you to the difference.

Two key emotions you may be experiencing can lead to uncharacteristic or unhealthy responses. The first is stress, the second, anger. Both are normal and natural in this situation, but each can lead you down dangerous paths. Sometimes you don't know you're acting in a self-destructive way until someone else, or maybe several others, points it out. Emotional stress of a certain magnitude can cause men to dive into themselves instead of reaching out for help. Says family counsellor Alyson Schafer: "It's not unusual to see men going through a split dealing with their stress in unhealthy ways. When feeling down, men are less likely to talk to other men or seek help generally, and therefore more likely to cope in unhealthy ways — poor eating, drinking, overworking, and so on."

It's true that, though my generation of men may be considered more emotionally intelligent than previous ones, we still have trouble admitting to difficult feelings, or processing those feelings with others. We tend to retreat into ourselves rather than opening up, and this withdrawal instinct can lead us to dark places that may in turn produce harmful urges, toward ourselves or even others. I did not experience such hazardous urges often, but it might be more accurate to say that I wasn't aware of whether I did. To say I might not have recognized them is not to say they weren't present. In fact, these kinds of impulses became, at some level, part of an up-and-down cycle that had previously been foreign to me. The degree of stress caused by the family rupture was immense, and my ability to maintain mental or emotional equanimity plummeted. I was miles away from the happy path. I know at one point Dustin asked me, "Daddy, why do you keep exhaling hard like that?" When I asked him what he meant, he told me that several times per day I would take a giant breath in and then a powerful one out. I didn't know I was doing it.

I remember one night in particular that I'd rather not talk about, but let me lay it on the line in the spirit of transparency. This was prior to my split, toward the end of the relationship. It was New Year's Eve. The details of the night aren't important, except to say that I drank to escape sadness for the first time in my life, and it scared me, a lot. I realized my mental burden was such that I was starting to do things I don't do. When things are really bad and you feel like you don't know how to get out from under the stress, you may find yourself exhibiting uncharacteristic behaviour.

I'm asking you to be careful, for the sake of your kids. Stress beyond a certain threshold can lead us to consider things we ought not to consider, because in the moment we'd rather feel anything other than what we're feeling. Your kids need a dad who is healthy and present. They need a dad who is sharp and aware. They need a dad who has energy and exuberance. On your worst days, in your worst moments, remember that the biggest favour you can do for them is to be the most awesome version of yourself you can be.

Anger can be an even more dangerous emotion than stress, for a simple reason. Most men I know experience plenty of stress in their normal lives, from various common sources — work, bills, taxes — and therefore have plenty of experience in dealing with it. For most people, these stressors are part of everyday life. But most guys I know are not angry types, and therefore are less used to dealing with this particular emotion, and alarmed by feeling it as much, and as intensely, as they might be after a split. "Anger can occur in response to many things," says Schafer. "Men often feel they're getting raped by the system, for example. So on top of the family breakup, there's the separation of income and property and maybe the feeling that she's disproportionately entitled, and that creates a whole other level of animosity, not just toward the ex but also toward her lawyer, the legal system, and so on."

Though I dislike admitting it, I can relate to what Schafer says. After my split I got angry, really angry, many times. I'm not an angry guy. I'm a cheerful, optimistic one. Or at least I thought I was. But boy did I get angry. Often I found I barely recognized the guy in the mirror because of the anger in his eyes, on his skin, in the tightness of his lips. I hated looking at that guy because I didn't know him, and I was frightened not so much by the thought of having turned into someone different as by the possibility that the guy in the mirror had taken over the other me forever.

As I said, for the most part I'm not sure I was aware of when I was in control or when I wasn't. I knew when I was stressed, but probably not how much. I knew when I became angry, but probably not to what extent. Often it took something like catching a glimpse of that guy in the mirror to stop me in my tracks and help me understand that something insidious was going on. With the benefit of hindsight, here are some signals that you may be getting a bit out of control:

- **You're less tolerant.** I'd be willing to bet you have, like me, a pretty long tripwire. But I also wouldn't be surprised if you're experiencing shorter nerve endings at the moment. An example: spills or breaks in the kitchen usually don't bother you (anyone with kids knows these are a regular occurrence), but suddenly you've started to have surprisingly big reactions when they occur.

- **You're taking more chances.** You're ordinarily a cautious driver, but lately you've been trying to beat red lights more often and not bothering to put on your seat belt. You find yourself more drawn to activities like skydiving, boxing, or base jumping. You've started playing online poker or betting significant sums on sporting events. You're sending flirtatious texts to married women or starting to wonder whether it would be so bad to answer one of those webcam girls who pop up whenever you visit a porn site. Be careful. Stop at the red light. Put your seat belt on.

- **You're less aware.** Well, not really, but it seems like you are, because you're breaking stuff, like glasses or plates, more often than usual, and seem to be encountering physical hazards with greater frequency. You're surprised at how often you seem to walk into the corner of a wall or an open cupboard door, just from going fast and not being aware that it was there. You're as focused and disciplined as ever in your Muay Thai class, but then you nearly get creamed crossing the intersection because you didn't notice the light was red.

- **You're more aggressive.** Ordinarily, if someone honks at you, you say something like "That guy must be having a hard day." Now you respond by rolling down the window and telling the guy to go screw himself, half-hoping that he'll want to throw down. When I play sports, I'm an intense competitor but a pretty big pacifist. But at the end of my first hockey season after my split, I remember seeing that my penalty minutes were highest on the team. I also realized I'd spent most of my time in the penalty box shouting, swearing, and challenging other players, or sometimes the ref. I remembered jokes my teammates had made about my having turned from a sniper into a goon. At the time I didn't realize this transformation was happening.

While it's important you and your kids stay safe, it's also important you cut yourself some slack. Of course, avoid violent or stupid acts, but also admit it's okay to have moments of mental weakness and emotional vulnerability. Your being less in control than usual makes sense right now. You're deeply agitated, mentally, emotionally, and psychically. You may not be behaving the way you'd normally behave, because life at the moment is not normal. Just because we're grown-ups doesn't mean we don't react. Often we react worse than our kids. You're going through this as a family. No one is immune to the internal grief that can translate into potentially dangerous behaviours. It's just that, because kids live in a smaller, more contained world, when they act out, their behaviour tends not to have far-reaching consequences. You live within a wider sphere. Your acting out in the wrong ways can have ramifications that are much worse.

No two people act out in the same way — no two kids, no two moms, no two dads. You've seen a dozen movie scenes in which the female lead, distraught about something (usually having been dumped by the guy she liked) is visited by a friend who finds her in her pyjamas, hair unkempt, eating ice cream straight from the tub. As men, our proverbial tub of ice cream may take many different forms, but suffice to say, deep emotional and spiritual pain can make us do some out-of-the-norm stuff in response. Like I said, I'm normally a non-violent person, but there were many times during the period of my separation when I felt like … I don't know, I felt like doing lots of things. It doesn't matter what. The point is I felt like

Three Episodes That Could Have Gone Much Worse but Thankfully Didn't

I like to think of myself as pretty responsible and, for the most part, as someone who exhibits self-control. But there were at least three incidents during the immediate aftermath of my split that showed I was not my normal self. Of note, each incident occurred while I was behind the wheel of a car.

- I was backing out of a spot in my parents' parking garage to go see the kids. I heard a crunch and felt myself jolted. I'd reversed straight into a concrete pillar. I got out of the car and looked at my rear fender, which was severely dented. I would have been really angry about the repair cost I'd just caused myself if I hadn't been so worried about the fact that I'd never even thought about the pillar being there.
- I was driving the kids to a birthday party at a farm north of the city. We were already late and I was tense because we also had to leave the party early to get somewhere else. Driving too fast along the two-lane country highway, I realized I was traveling in the wrong direction, wasting more time. In frustration I told the kids I'd made a mistake and then pulled a U-turn. Almost immediately, I saw flashing lights in my rear-view. Feeling like I was going to explode, I explained to the kids that I was being pulled over, and this would be a good experience for them because everyone gets pulled over.

    Alisha said, "Daddy, do you have to go to jail?" I assured her I wouldn't. The cop took my licence and registration and went back to his cruiser to check my records. Now I was making us even later for the party, increasing my agitation. The cop returned, handed me back my documents, and said, "You know you nearly T-boned me back there." He looked concerned.

No, I didn't know I'd almost T-boned him. I didn't know that at all. I realized I'd been aware of little other than my own anger and irritation when I made that move. His eyes, his tone, and his decision not to give me a ticket gave me pause. A long one.

- I hate even thinking about this incident, much less writing about it, but I want to be candid. I had taken all three kids, as well as my nephew David, out for lunch, and we were getting back in the car. I started driving away. After, I don't know, maybe two seconds, I heard David yell, "Alisha!" She was standing fifteen feet behind the car, now crying and in hysterics.

  I stopped the car and ran out and took her in my arms and apologized and calmed her down. I can barely talk about how consumingly guilty and self-hating this episode made me feel. I've had to face the fact again and again that I drove away *without thinking about who was or wasn't in the car*. I just started going. I might as well have been unconscious. In some measure, I probably was. I've had recurring nightmares about Alisha being partially in the car and being dragged along, or standing behind the car and my reversing into her.

  That evening I went back over the situation endlessly, recognizing that I hadn't really been thinking about anything when I started to pull away. I tucked Alisha in, squeezed her tightly, and apologized over and over while she was still awake. Then I watched her sleep for a long time, kissed her forehead and cheek and nose, and apologized another dozen times before leaving her bedroom. In the bathroom, I looked at myself in the mirror and forced myself to say, "You started driving away without Alisha today. You didn't know it until David shouted. You aren't well. You drove away without Alisha. Something very bad could have happened. Do you understand?" I haven't done anything like that since.

doing them, and none would have been good. Ultimately, I made passage from that place of emotional darkness and severe mental strain to one of renewed light and better inner balance. Several things were responsible for facilitating this shift.

- **Having close calls.** Please don't wait until something irretrievably stupid happens for you to wake up to the fact you might not be yourself. Dangerous moments like the first two I described from my own life (see sidebar) helped me understand that the current I.J. was in certain instances not the regular I.J. The third moment was like a bucket of ice water dumped on my heart. I'm grateful these incidents didn't have worse results and hauntingly aware that they could have.
- **Starting to dislike myself.** After a while I realized I wasn't enjoying my own company, so it was hard to imagine others were. Your friends will always be in your corner, but that doesn't mean they'll enjoy hanging around with you if all you can talk about is how evil your ex is, how annoying

divorce is, or how angry you are. You have to make a choice. I didn't quite see it in myself until others pointed it out, especially my parents, who told me I was often unrecognizable in disposition and temperament. I decided to make an active and conscious effort to recapture my real self and manage the stress and anger in pieces rather than let it infiltrate my internal spirit and external behaviour.

- **Choosing my battles.** There is, to put it in technical terms, a shitload of stuff to deal with when you separate. And almost no way to get through that stuff quickly or simply. Practically speaking, the daily process of splitting can take up your entire schedule; mentally speaking, it can occupy your entire headspace. It's important you try not to let it. When I talk about choosing your battles, I'm not just refer- ring to arguments with your ex. I'm also talking about bat- tles with yourself. You can spend this entire period stewing and steaming, huffing and puffing, railing and venting, which will leave you feeling constantly drained, or you can choose to, and learn to, disengage both externally and internally, in healthy ways, at regular intervals. Sometimes the battle is necessary, but most of the time it's not.

- **Learning self-removal.** You're an adult, so you can handle a lot, but you're also a human being, so you have a breaking point. When I asked Winnipeg therapist Lindsey Jay Walsh the top three pieces of advice he would give dads for main- taining a positive relationship with their kids during and after a split, his first piece of advice was "Show up," echoing the top rule of so many others. His second, also reinforcing the guidance of others, was "Be bigger, stronger, and kind, as much and as often as you can." (For ideas on how to practise kindness, see Chapter 11.) His last was this: "And if you need a Daddy time out, figure out a safe way to do it."

Isn't that interesting? I wouldn't have expected it. But when I reflected on my own behaviour, I realized how often I felt myself starting to get to a point where the stress and tension were so great that the most helpful thing I could do was to take a step back, which sometimes meant removing myself from the situation. Don't feel guilty if you can't handle everything that's coming at you right now. As Walsh says, sometimes your healthiest move is to step away and Zen out. Use active techniques like meditation, deep breathing, yoga, or positive visualization to take a short respite, then re-enter the situation when you feel ready.

- **Experiencing love.** Fulvia and I went through our family breakups more or less in parallel. Individually, we sometimes bore sadness or bitterness toward our exes or about the overall process during different stages. In many instances I felt frustrated, angry, or exasperated, and she had to buoy me up or talk me down, and in many others the situation was reversed. But as a couple, our mutual flow of affection, devotion, respect, and deep genuine caring was the raft we rode together down a winding and volatile river. In even the most challenging moments of the family split, I was uplifted by the joy of our relationship and sustained by the depth of our bond. On the darkest of days, love continued to soar.

- **Giving it time.** Don't kill me, but, yes, time. Interactions with my ex went from us being burning mad all the time, to highly frustrated a great deal of the time, to fairly cordial with the occasional blow-up. My family situation went from "All hell's broken loose" to prevalent sadness and gloom to "Everyone is themselves again," even though we're still dealing with stuff. My personal circumstances went from "This can't be real: I'm not seeing my kids every morning" to "Lord, my parents' condo is so far, but maybe we'll look back and see this as an adventure one day" to "Gosh, I'm so happy the kids love my place and think of it as one of their two homes." The alarming guy I saw in the mirror so full of ire and potential for scary behaviour has, thankfully, gone away, replaced by the one I knew before. I still have lots of stress, but for the most part it's just the normal, how-can-I-keep-up-with-expenses stress of everyday life, which I welcome with open arms compared to the previous feeling.

Don't get me wrong. I don't want to make it sound as though I'm centred and chill all the time. My advising you to do things like step away from highly tense and stressful moments is also a continual reminder to myself. While working on this very chapter, I had an exchange with my ex that consisted of about three texts each and was accompanied by the following internal monologue:

> Come on, not now. I was in such a good mood.
>
> Damn it. I'm getting steamed. I don't want to get steamed. Okay, just respond — it'll be worse to leave it. There. Good answer. Very fair and polite.
>
> There goes the blood pressure. Oh, hell, I can't believe how quickly this happens. Just stay calm. This is not worth getting mad about.
>
> I'm so mad.

What we were texting about is irrelevant. The purpose of my sharing this with you is just to say that, while I'm in a far more stable mental and emotional place than I was in the earlier stages of our split, I am also susceptible to moments in which the blood boils and I feel myself sliding toward a place that I know is unhealthy. So I'm still working on gaining equanimity too.

Way back in 1928, a gentleman named John A. Shedd wrote, "A ship in harbor is safe, but that is not what ships are built for." He was right. Humans are not ships that stay peacefully in their slips, because that's not life. We cast off every day and go out on the water. Sometimes the waters are familiar, sometimes unknown. Sometimes they're calm, sometimes choppy. Sometimes the surface looks placid, then a rogue wave rises up and crashes down on us. The only thing certain is that the current will never be the same two days in a row. We adjust because we have to.

I know you're in rough waters now, and you may want to shake your fist and yell at the sky. Remember, though, that your kids are in the boat with you, and you're riding out this storm together. Be safe yourself, so that you can keep a close watch on them. Don't do it for me, and don't do it for you. Do it for them.

Ten Questions: My Mate Angelo

What were the biggest mistakes you made with your kids during your split, and how have you addressed them?

The biggest mistake I made was to take shots at my ex in the presence of my kids. It wasn't until one of them told me to stop that I realized it was negatively affecting them. For many years now, I have stopped this behaviour, and even find myself complimenting their mother and stressing how important it is that they treat her with the love and respect she deserves.

What's been your greatest challenge?

Not seeing my kids every day. I do not miss living with my ex, but I really do miss being part of a family. I miss having breakfast with my kids in the morning and dinner with them in the evening. I miss kissing them goodnight and hanging out with them every day. I make sure to either call them each day or at least text them several times a day so I feel connected to them and know what's happening in their lives. And on the days they're with me, I make sure I'm available, not out with friends or working. Even if it's just sitting with them at the table while they do their homework, I make sure they know I'm there and dedicated to them.

Can you describe your lowest or hardest moments with your kids?

After my split I moved into a two-bedroom apartment. My lowest point was when my son said he didn't want to stay with me anymore because he had to share a room with his two sisters. He had just turned sixteen, and I knew he had a valid point and that this day was going to come. We talked about it and realized there was room in the apartment where we could put his mattress and create a space of his own. This was good for my daughters too. All is well now.

How about moments when you saw light at the end of the tunnel?
I've just started a new job after bouncing around for four years, a year and a half of those being unemployed. Having an income and a purpose has lifted my spirits. Money is still tight, so I can't do all the things I'd like to do with my kids, but as I start to make more money, I see us being able to do more things with each other, like we used to before the split.

In your view, what do kids need most from their dad during or after a breakup?
Love, reassurance, time, togetherness, patience, understanding, and the ability to have a good working relationship with their mother. It's also important to have aligned parenting patterns. While I might not agree with everything my ex says or does, I have to uphold similar values and ways of bringing up our children.

How much emotion did you show your kids with regard to your split? Where do you stand on how much "real" they should see versus how much they should be protected?
As mentioned before, I often used to take shots at my ex in front of the kids, which was a bad move. That doesn't happen anymore, and it has ensured a much more loving and caring relationship with them. They saw enough "real" when we lived together as a couple. They don't need to see it anymore.

What would you say are the key hurdles to get over as a family before kids can start adjusting to the new normal?
Kids need to understand that they now have two separate homes — not one home and "Dad's place." Kids need to be made to feel

comfortable that none of this was their fault. Kids need to be reassured that even though Mom and Dad couldn't live together anymore, they both love them just the same as always. Kids need to see their parents getting along. It often takes a lot of patience, but in the long run, it's worth it to see the children more relaxed and comfortable.

How do you handle the practical issues of two households?

Anyone can get used to anything. I still don't like dropping the kids off at their mom's after a nice weekend together though. I think they actually handle it better than I do. There's a lot of alone time when they aren't home with me, but I try not to let them see how much it hurts me to leave them for a few days at a time. I don't use any specific methods. I just try to spend as much quality time with them as possible when we're together. My ex works now and often isn't home even when it's her time with them. I make it a point that when they're with me, we're together. Having said that, I'm no longer insistent that they be with me on my days and weekends. They have lives filled with friends and school and extracurricular activities, and they are free to come and go as they like.

What are your top three pieces of advice to other dads for maintaining a loving and healthy relationship with their kids after a split?

One, be as flexible as possible. Don't be stubborn. Don't dig your heels in as a default mode. No matter how much you dislike your ex, you need to find a way to maintain a positive relationship with her, especially in front of the children.

Two, be there for your kids. Don't put work or friends or a new girlfriend before your children. Even if you weren't a hands-on dad when you were living with your ex, recognize that your kids need you now more than ever.

Three, do your best to establish one consistent way of parenting, as much as you can. Be on the same page as your ex to the greatest extent possible, so that your children can see that, even though their parents are no longer together, they still agree on how to raise them.

7

Maintaining Your Fitness

The consensus among experts is that it takes two to three years for a family to regain some semblance of normalcy after a split. In the months following your breakup, you might feel like things are as far from normal as they can be. Which means there's a good chance you feel not only mentally washed out, but also physically numb. Worse, you may have the impression that you're scarcely in control of anything, a sense very different from the one you probably lived before — when you got up in, and came home to, the same place, the same bed, the same partner, and the same children every day. Now it suddenly feels like you've walked into a very dark and twisted episode of *The Twilight Zone* (okay, I guess they were all dark and twisted, but, you know, even more so). Or perhaps you feel you've somehow found yourself thrust into one of those carnival funhouses in which everything is stretched and warped and nothing is the way it should be. And that's on the good days.

It's true — there isn't much you can control during this period. You're trying to manage the highly intense emotions of multiple people, figure out complicated practical issues, provide innocent little people whom you love more than life itself answers to questions that have no good answers, and just get through the day emotionally unscathed, which happens seldom. But there are some things you can still control. One of them is your body. The other is your mind. The reason this chapter title refers to fitness is that, at a crossroads like the one you're at now, when you probably wish you could just crawl into bed, stay there, and turn off your brain for a few hours, or a few days, now is in fact a time when you need to be stronger than ever, both physically and mentally. To inspire you to be stronger, let me toss at you the wisdom of four gents:

"Take care of your body. It's the only place you have to live."

American entrepreneur and motivational speaker Jim Rohn said this, and was he ever right. Yes, the breakup process is really hard, and complicated, and tiring (or, as my son Cory would say, really suckish). But no matter what happens, you have only one body to live in, and one mind to use, and it's your duty, not only for yourself but also for your kids, to take care of both. The good news is that no matter how hard and complicated and tiring anything is …

"Life doesn't get easier or more forgiving, we get stronger and more resilient."

This gem is from the noted author and consultant (not to mention decorated military veteran) Steve Maraboli. Our human ability to endure is remarkable. Good thing, since you're really up against it right now, having to bring to bear all of your mental and physical resources just to get to the next day, which is probably going to kick you in the groin all over again. Endurance doesn't just happen, of course. I mean, yes, all kinds of people make it through stuff it seems they shouldn't, but those who do typically have the right kind of mental strength, physical fortitude, or both. We have to do the work. Let's go back to Mr. Rohn for a moment, who also said:

"Some things you have to do every day. Eating seven apples on Saturday night instead of one a day just isn't going to get the job done."

This wonderful insight has direct application to marital breakups, and what it takes to pull the people you love through them. The more we feel overwhelmed by our anguish or helplessness, the stronger our instinct to just hunker down and wait for the storm to blow over. But the better tactic is to face the storm head-on, with unyielding strength and unwavering resolve. This is a tempest, and it isn't going to pass like a sun shower in July. The clouds will lift eventually, but while the storm whistles and wails around you, you need to fortify yourself from the inside out. Putting this advice another way:

"If you don't do what's best for your body, you're the one who comes up on the short end."

This jewel was uttered by Julius Erving. He puts his sentiment in simple terms, and they are dead-on. I would never seriously compare the experience of a family split to preparing for a basketball game, but I will say that the more fit you are mentally and physically, the better disposed you are to face any demanding task, whether an NBA tilt or the marathon of pain and despair that is family breakup. Your family is the team, and the team will benefit enormously if you can demonstrate the strength and poise to lead them through.

––––––––––––

There's a reason I'm using the term *fitness* — as in wellness — in this chapter. I'm not talking about getting bigger pecs or tighter glutes, or adding points to your IQ. I'm talking about how important it is that you maintain a state of general good health, sufficient energy, and, especially, forward motion, as opposed to the opposite condition of malaise, resignation, and stagnancy.

At times, relinquishing your fitness will seem a simpler choice than continuing to marshal the strength you need every day. But relinquishing in mind can run parallel with relinquishing in body, aided by seductive means of making ourselves feel even worse than we already feel, like cookies, cake, chips, pizza, beer, and a host of other unhealthy crap. You may be the type of guy who is tough, who is resilient, who is a warrior, who has dealt with stuff. But the pain that accompanies a breakup can be killer, and it might make you want to say, "Screw it, I'm having a Big Mac supersize combo for breakfast, watching porn all day, then going to sleep."

Resist the urge to retreat into a literal and figurative cave. Here are five reasons:

- **You need to be alert.** I don't need to tell you that, as a parent, you have dozens of decisions to make every day, and the swiftness and precision with which you make them can often have large ramifications for your kids. Keep your edge.
- **You need to be able to focus.** Unfortunately, your job doesn't care that life is shitty right now, and neither do your bills. You need to keep doing your job and doing it well, and that requires concentration and keenness. Constant sugar comas do not help.
- **You need energy.** Boy, do you. On top of what you usually require energy for — doing your job, buying groceries, helping your kids with their homework and taking them to extracurricular activities, seeing your family, getting exercise, maintaining cooking, cleaning, and laundry — right now you need extra reserves of vigour and vitality, both to manage your own emotional and practical journey through the split and (in turn) to help your kids cope with theirs. What you do *not* need is energy from artificial sources, like anabolic steroids or other such substances. It's a short road from taking these once to building a dependency on them, which can have severe implications. Find the boost you need from the natural sources all around you, especially your children.
- **You need to be attractive.** I'm saying this not only because you're single now and will likely want to find a new partner at some point. (This is an important consideration, though. Commit to getting, or staying, in shape and looking your best. Almost half of marriages end, so you're back in a pool with a lot of people, which means there's competition.) The main purpose of being attractive isn't to look good to potential partners, however. It's that:

- **Your kids need to see you healthy.** While researching this book, I talked to many adults whose parents had split when they were kids. In response to my question "What helped you get through it?" many said that as kids they felt they could start to move on when they saw their parents moving on. More specifically, many of them described to me the fear they had experienced seeing their larger-than-life dad suddenly slump-shouldered, despondent, and without passion. Each of them seemed to describe something like a less-present, less-alive version of the man they'd known. And each told me that when their dad started to seem to come back into himself, it gave them back the feeling of security and assurance that had, along with him, started to diminish.

  Sometimes they described this experience in practical terms. One said, "I got so sad the first time I entered his basement apartment with no furniture, but then when he got a normal place and started feeling happier and more confident, it allowed me to breathe a little." Other times they described their experience in emotional terms. Another said, "He used to make me laugh all the time, throw me in the air, make up games, play music, but then he just got flat, like all the air went out of him for a while. But at a certain point it was like the oxygen started to come back into him, and that's what let me start to move on too." Some parts of divorce are complicated, but some are pretty simple. The matter of fitness is simple. Your kids take their cues from you.

Now, listen: I'm not saying don't be genuine. Yes, it's healthy for your kids to see the real you, including the fact that you are not in fact invincible, immortal, or cheerful all the time. As Dr. Rotem Regev says:

> By far, the biggest mistake I see dads making is trying to act as if everything is normal. It's not. Something big happened, and it's going to be a while until a new

normal sets in. Your kids sense this in their bodies, in their hearts. By pretending everything is normal, you invalidate their experience. When kids' experience is invalidated, they learn not to trust themselves or their feelings. They may start to mistrust what they hear from you, and believe that something is indeed wrong, or different, and the road from that to their believing it's their fault is a short one.

Psychotherapist Kyle Karalash agrees: "Maintain honesty and don't be scared to show your emotions. If you're feeling upset, you don't need to hide it. Children want to know they can go to their parents to talk about upsetting things. I hear from teenagers that they wish they could share vulnerabilities with their parents, that they wish it was less intimidating. Being a parent is hard work and can be emotional. You're human and you make mistakes. Model how to manage and interact with those mistakes and emotions."

On the other hand, you're the adult here, and you have coping skills your children have not yet developed. As Toronto psychologist Andrew Shaul says, "Be honest to a point and let them see you're human, but still be the adult and parent. Their world is shaken, and they need your stability. If you send the message that you're going to be okay, they can feel they're going to be okay. But if you look like you're falling to pieces, they're going to think, 'If Dad's falling apart, what about us?'"

The experts seem to agree that every word you say and every act you do has a profound effect on your kids. They also seem to agree that it would be false to project to your kids constant happiness through what everyone knows is a time of intense sadness. But they also appear aligned to the view that, while allowing your kids a dose of reality is fair, you also need to be their dad — keeping them organized, holding them when they cry, watching their games and recitals, taking their slings and arrows.

So what's the right equation? What's the perfect formula of vulnerability versus strength, emotion versus composure, telling them stuff versus telling them nothing? What's the balance between being real versus protecting them? The best take on this was articulated to me by

Alyson Schafer, who says you need to acknowledge the family grief you're experiencing but also to exhibit to your kids that you're solid. "It's okay to show some emotion and talk about the situation in real terms," she says, "but also to show that you're in control. It's dangerous for either parent to look like they've been worn down, beaten up, or victimized by the process. Kids look to their parents to see if things are okay, and therefore if they themselves are. You need to show strength, confidence, and self-possession, through your body language, the way you move, the way you talk. Whichever way you behave, they will internalize." She calls parents demonstrating their strength "leadership of the family" and uses the analogy of a pilot flying a plane.

> I would say that it's fair to say to your kids, "We're really sad," because it's a grieving process, and you're all going through that sense of loss together. But imagine you're on an airplane, and the pilot comes on the loudspeaker sobbing and talking about what an awful day he's had, and then he says, by the way, we'll be taking off in a few minutes. You do not want to be on that airplane, because you have no confidence in him piloting it. The family is the airplane, the kids are the passengers, and you as parents need to be the pilots. It's up to you to help them believe, "They broke up, but he's okay, and she's okay, so I guess I'm going to be okay."

Besides reassuring them, there's another important reason you need to show your kids that leadership. They have questions about what's going on, and if they feel you're too closed off or too distressed to be there for them, they will only feel more alienated from the process, as opposed to being able to come to terms with it.

"I've noticed a pattern in which children begin to feel as though they need to walk on eggshells around their parents," says Kyle Karalash. "I've worked with children who didn't feel comfortable sharing their feelings because they already saw their parents as overwhelmed. These children ended up trying to deal with their thoughts, feelings, and questions on their own. They expressed a buildup of anger, frustration, or worry that they would ultimately be rejected by their parents. This can stem from the stress of not being in the loop."

Staying healthy will allow you to be present for your kids during the most harrowing period of their lives. For every dad, this means something different. But make the commitment to doing it.

Here are some common questions I've been asked by other dads, and the answers that I think make sense.

I already work out regularly. Given this is a time of change, do you think I should switch up my routine?

You should *always* be mixing up your routine, no matter what else is going on in your life. As any expert will tell you, doing the same type of workout in the same way at the same intensity quickly loses effect, because our bodies are so good at learning new things and habituating to them. You may have heard this referred to as "plateauing." Always give your body new challenges to try and different ways to use itself. If you've only ever lifted weights, try hitting the pool. If you're accustomed strictly to distance running, give barbells a shot. If you never stray from the treadmill because it's comfortable and familiar, force yourself to take a boxing or judo class. Nothing benefits the body more than variation. Your mind will appreciate it too.

I usually work out at home. Now that I'm single, should I join a gym as a place to meet people?

While I do know a few couples who met at the gym, I don't know many. Gyms aren't necessarily conducive places to meet potential partners. Most people who go to the gym do so to carry out a specific routine in a focused and efficient way, without distraction. The majority of those I speak to, when I ask them what they want out of their gym time, tell me they are there to devote their energy and concentration to the task at hand, and are generally not there to chat with others.

That said, I'm describing the traditional gym: benches and dumbbells and mats and machines, people listening to their tunes and swigging from their water bottles while feeling the personal burn and enjoying their own endorphin high. In other words, I think that, for most, working out at the gym is a largely self-focused pursuit to satisfy individual need.

However, beyond the typical gym setting are plenty of physical activities that do lend themselves well to social connection. Ultimate Frisbee. CrossFit. Yoga classes. Pilates. Running or cycling groups. Tough Mudder. Tennis. Golf. Co-ed softball. All of these satisfy the exercise need, but they also involve continual and direct interaction with other like-minded people.

Given how generally bummed I am at the moment, I don't feel much motivation to move. What should I do?

You should stop thinking about it and — apologies to Nike — just do it. Stop reading this right now and do twenty pushups and twenty jumping jacks. Go run around the block. Put on a sitcom and move your body, in any way at all, from the beginning of the episode to the end. You said you feel bummed, right? Exercise is the most reliable un-bumming thing you can do, and the easiest, because you can do it anywhere at any time. Don't think about the things you're feeling that make you not want to get off the couch or out of bed; think about how you know you feel during, and after, exercise. Even five minutes of intense stretching or flexing will make you feel great. (Don't believe me? Flex both biceps as hard as you can for ten seconds.)

For me, the number-one motivation is to exercise alongside your kids. First, it's critically important for them to see you staying in shape, and in motion. Second, working out together is a fun and unique bonding activity. Finally, it's a great way to help your kids expend energy (which is a welcome alternative to realizing only at bedtime that they're still hyper because they didn't move enough during the day). Here are three ideas for exercising together:

- **Pleasurable push-ups.** Push-ups are a great exercise because they can be done anywhere and you don't need any equipment to do them. Your younger kids will love it if you ask them to get on your back while you try to crank out a set. Or you can reverse it and lie on your back while trying to press them up like a barbell. Or stand up, hoist them into your arms, and use them to do biceps curls. Your older kids may enjoy doing push-ups with you — maybe even seeing who can do more, or coming up with creative spins on the traditional movement. One of my favourite moments following my split was Alisha arriving home from school one day and saying, "Daddy, I thought of the best push-up challenge! Can I show you?"

- **Joint jogging.** Kids of any age love running with their parents. They love to show you how fast they can run and how far they can go. They love it when you challenge them, treating them like serious athletes, and they love it equally (or more) when you introduce some goofiness into the activity. (Who can run backward the fastest? Who can do the best sprints-mixed-with-cartwheels? Who can finish a full lap of the track while singing the entire time?) You might be surprised how much energy you can burn just by having fun.

- **Creative contests.** My kids adore when I take them to the park and issue them physical challenges, at increasing levels of difficulty, using the equipment and nature sur- rounding us. Level 1, for example, might entail jumping onto a park bench with one foot, twirling around, then jumping off and sticking the landing on the opposite foot. Subsequent levels might involve spinning on a piece of playground equipment while having to catch and throw back a tennis ball, scaling a play structure in a set amount of time, or climbing a tree. Sometimes I'll design an obstacle course for them. I demonstrate each move and/or join the competition myself so that we all get exercise (in their case, without even thinking about it). The combina- tion of the outdoor environment, the fun and exhilaration of the competition, and their natural inclination to want to show me what they can achieve makes this tremendous fun every time.

Regardless of how you choose to embark on, or maintain, your fitness journey, don't do it completely on your own. "Get support for yourself," says Regev. "Talk to friends, go to therapy, try meditation, get active, book a massage. Make sure you feel taken care of. You can't pour from an empty cup."

Men tend to resist such advice. I wouldn't be surprised if you read the sentence at the end of the previous paragraph and silently scoffed. With each generation, I like to think we're getting a little better at admitting our feelings, sharing them with each other, and accepting the support of others. However, as men, we do still often revert to lone-wolf mentality, especially in the face of something we feel may be embarrassing or shameful. It may help you to think of any help you seek as help you're seeking not only for yourself, but for your kids as well, since the more whole you can be, the stronger a dad they have to help guide them through the storm.

"If you're having negative feelings," says Shaul, "if you're hurt, or angry, or sad, deal with those feelings away from your kids, and make yourself as well as you can. Don't just think, okay, they're upset, I'm upset, we're all going to be upset together. Get support so that, when you're with your kids, they don't need to be involved in helping you cope. Get the help you need so that, when you're with them, you can be your best self."

Be your best self. Remember that. Take care of your body. Take care of your mind. The harder it may feel to do so, the more important it is. Be strong and sharp for your kids now so that, when the clouds eventually lift, you can appreciate the rainbow together.

Some Frank Words from My Pal Larry

The emotional pain of the family breakup devastated me. Even though I'd seen the writing on the wall some months prior, when my wife told me she wanted a divorce, I was heartbroken. I wondered how it could have happened, how we'd gotten there, and what my role had been in it. At first I blamed her, but through therapy and time, I was able to see that I'd had a part in the marital breakdown too, if not necessarily the breakup.

Still, I felt angry, hurt, and betrayed. The anxiety and stress took a horrible toll: I lost forty pounds in about a month. The immediate aftermath is still a haze. I don't remember what or how we told the kids. I only remember a feeling of sinking. My kids were very young, so, in some ways, it was easier than situations in which the kids are older. Their habits and patterns could be more easily adapted. Nonetheless, they kept asking for many years why we couldn't work it out, and we kept telling them simply that sometimes parents are better off as friends.

After the split I made sure to make myself even more accessible to my kids, both physically and emotionally. The more time I spent with them, the more I realized that what they needed most was to know it wasn't their fault. Spending time together was the best medicine. In over eight years as a single parent, I hired a babysitter only four times. Otherwise, the 50 percent of the time that they were with me, we were together. I knew they needed to know that I was there and that I would never disparage their mother, even if at times I hated her. No matter what, I always treated her respectfully in front of the kids. They deserved that from me.

At first I felt like a grand piano had been dropped on my heart. I felt lost, emasculated, useless. Since I had always seen myself and measured my self-esteem through my wife's eyes, I was shattered. I didn't have any real sense of my own self-worth. I basically stayed home and wallowed in self-pity. I felt insignificant and insecure and couldn't bear to see anyone.

After a while I swung in the other direction, going out too often, just to avoid being alone and the hurt that would come with it. After a few months of that stupidity, I realized I needed to get comfortable with myself. I started to work out daily, which I found calming and centring. I went to therapy, allowing me perspective and a place to vent. I read a ton of books, helping me self-examine and self-actualize. I accepted the support of family and friends, helping me slowly deal with the stress and pain. All of this helped me better understand myself and achieve my own sense of worth. Finally I came to feel at ease with who, and where, I was.

8

Embracing Your Friends and Family

In prosperity, our friends know us; in adversity, we know our friends.
— JOHN CHURTON COLLINS

There's a strange paradox you may find yourself experiencing during a family split. The positive part: you're probably realizing how many people care about you, at least if the constant texts, calls, and emails are any indication. The negative part: you don't really feel like seeing or talking to anybody, because you feel lost and helpless, you don't like the dark cloud you're carrying around, and your tank is constantly empty. Friends, co-workers, and family members may want to help; you want to hide. There are plenty of reasons for the way you feel, all understandable. You don't want to tell your sob story over and over. You don't want to bring others down. You don't want to seem like a loser or a failure. You don't want to sound weak or self-pitying. You don't need everyone and their dog to see you cry.

Although it's natural to want to avoid contact at a time like this, your friends and family are kind, safe, healthy outlets for you. This group occupies a special place and has unique status during your time of greatest struggle, because it consists of people who want to be there just to provide an ear or a shoulder, without judgment or opinion. They have no agenda and are asking nothing in return. They simply care. So try to let them in.

In a way, also paradoxically, you may feel like you want to talk to everyone and no one. You may feel you'd like to vent to the whole world and at the same time keep things to yourself. On certain days you may feel like your situation is the worst ever and you need to share it just to get it off your chest; on other days you may feel ashamed to complain about your problems because far worse ones exist all over the world. Loss of the former family structure gives rise to these odd dichotomies, which come from the aforementioned internal conflict: the need to share versus the instinct to hide. Let's talk about how to strike the balance between having the alone time you need just to feel what you feel, and spending time in the presence of those who care for you unconditionally.

"I value the friend who for me finds time on his calendar," wrote American aphorist Robert Brault, "but I cherish the friend who for me does not consult his calendar." True friends are defined in part by the fact that they seem to be part of all of your positive and special memories, but they're defined even more by the way they materialize at the most difficult times. They don't ask questions; they just show up.

Everyone will be calling you and asking you to talk, to go for a beer, to party, to let loose, to hit the clubs, to take in a ballgame. As I've said, you may feel an impulse in total contrast to their desire to provide support: the urge to curl up in a dark room and stay there. This is, many experts believe, a gender-based and socially reinforced instinct. "With men, there's a huge taboo around loneliness," says therapist Dr. Rotem Regev. "Even dads who initiated the separation because they felt lonely in the relationship often feel very lonely afterwards. They may experience themselves withdrawing from others, not letting even close friends know how sad they are. In our Western culture, it's more common for women to get together with friends and express their emotions. Sadness is rarely shared among men. This is a vicious cycle: dads feel lonely yet keep to themselves, making them feel lonelier still."

The presence of friends and family is good for you because they're like therapists while being sources of enjoyment at the same time. They know you best, want nothing other than to be there, and they charge nothing. As William Shakespeare wrote, "A friend is one that knows you as you are, understands where you have been, accepts what you have become, and still, gently allows you to grow."

Here's an account of the best therapy session I ever had. My friend Dave and I have played baseball together for many years. During the spring when my split was occurring, and things were just like a different nightmare every day, I wasn't doing much other than trying to get through the day at work, staying connected to the kids, sleeping when possible, and keeping in shape by hitting the gym at strange hours. I stopped my usual routine of playing hockey and baseball a few times a week because I was too depressed and didn't think it was fair to let my teammates see me this way. They knew me as someone very different from the way I felt, looked, during this time. Dave wrote to me, insisting I come to the next baseball game. He told me to arrive before the other guys. We could talk, he said, or toss the ball around, or jog, whatever.

Reluctantly, I went. Even the feeling of putting on the uniform was positive, slinging the bag over my shoulder, driving to the diamond. Dave was there when I arrived. He gave me a hug that made we want to cry, then we sat on the grass, and I guess at some point I just started talking. He asked a couple of questions and offered some insights that no one else could have because no one knows me like he does or shares the same history. We put on our gloves and started to play catch. There was no resolution reached, no answers offered. It was simply the kind of catharsis that comes from having an intimate chat with a close friend who makes you feel safe and understood.

The most important thing about your friends and family members is that they don't care about the circumstances of your split or who did what. In the words of Canadian educator Laurence J. Peter, "You can always tell a real friend: when you've made a fool of yourself he doesn't feel you've done a permanent job."

We never got to play our game that day. As the other guys started to arrive at the field, the skies opened. This somehow seemed a positive metaphor. While everyone else took shelter under the trees, I went out and started running the bases. The rain came in sheets. My uniform was soaked, the water bouncing off the brim of my cap, my cleats waterlogged. And I loved it. I felt free and happy, if only for that moment, those minutes. Most of the guys on both teams eventually left. I continued to run.

Later Dave wrote to ask if I was all right. He mistakenly thought that my running in the torrent represented my being lost and in despair. What he didn't know was that the chat with him beforehand had allowed me to release myself into that moment of pleasure — the rain pounding my body, the glistening wet grass, the vibrant smell of the trees, the stormy sky. It was those few minutes with a dear friend that had opened me up again to feeling alive and present. I explained this to Dave and thanked him, telling him my running the bases in the lashing rain had not been a sign of me going away, it had been a sign of me coming back. And that had happened just from talking to him, my lifelong friend.

To me the conventional idea of "support" is sometimes assumed to mean formal therapy, when in fact there are many different activities that may help, from running to relaxing, sleeping to having sex. The best support I've found is the unconditional love shown by friends and family.

In the midst of a family breakup, it's natural to find yourself feeling opposing emotional needs simultaneously: the contact of others, and the desire to be insulated. Often I felt like I wanted to talk to everybody and nobody. Everybody, because I hoped one of them might have the magic insight to show me a sliver of light. Nobody, because I felt my story sounded dumb, selfish, common, or juvenile, and I couldn't stand the sound of my own voice telling it.

You need to find the balance that works for you. Be honest with others about where you're at and what you're feeling, so that, even when you're declining offers to go for dinner, you're still maintaining lines of communication. Writing to your buddy to explain why you don't feel up to getting together can be as therapeutic as getting together, simply from the act of connecting. It's also, as I discovered in my situation with Dave, kind to assure them that, even though you may not be as physically present as usual, you're still there.

No matter how low you feel, take the time to thank the people who call you, check in on you, do little things to pick you up or make you smile. Each of these gestures is another small stone placed in the river to help you make passage.

Above all, don't let yourself detach completely. Like despondency, seclusion can become a habit. It's at the times when we have the strongest instinct to shrink away that it's most important not to. In his book *The Happiness Advantage*, Shawn Achor describes how intense pressure can cause us to pull inward at times when we in fact need our friends and family most. He used, as one test group, his students at Harvard. What he observed was that, rather than using their social supports, these students instead showed a tendency to isolate themselves. They were, as he describes it, "too stressed to reach out for love." Faced with such high amounts of pressure, they had "compromised the very support systems they so ardently needed."

When you're blue, sometimes talking to friends is like going to the gym: you don't feel like going at first, but you're glad you did it after. As Marcus Tullius Cicero put it, "Friendship improves happiness and abates misery, by the doubling of our joy and the dividing of our grief." That isn't just a cool thought from an early Roman philosopher and statesman. It's also empirically true: our social support network is one of the most powerful predictors of success and happiness. My sister wrote or called me virtually every day to check in, offer support, and assure me things were going to improve in time. Her voice was a thread of security and faith that she ensured was constant, and she helped divide my grief.

While writing this book, I had countless conversations with dads willing to talk privately about their sorrow. This parade of loving but desperate dads showed me that the best kind of help comes not from the stereotypical compensatory acts of buying a sports car or trying to have sex with twentysomethings, but from connecting with others and discovering you are not alone. Figure out what degree and frequency of interaction feels right for you. If you feel like a mess, you may feel that spending time with others, even briefly, only represents a mess of a different sort. You may feel that talking about your situation with others will only burden them, yet not talking about your situation is insincere. You may find yourself feeling uncomfortable in situations that are supposed to be normal, or thinking that all eyes and ears are on you when you'd rather just be invisible.

In fact, none of these feelings is relevant, and none of these perceptions is true. Your friends and family don't need an agenda for a conversation with you, or a template for knowing how to show you support. Be honest about when and why you may need to hide from the world a bit, but don't hide completely or permanently. Allow yourself the time to be with your pain and grief, but don't make it your best friend to the exclusion of those who love you and know you best. Spill your guts or say nothing. Discuss the intricacies of family law or just go see a movie. Cry your eyes out and yell until you're hoarse or meditate on the mystery of life. What you do together doesn't matter to your friends and family; they just want to be there for you, in whatever context or setting, as caring voices, familiar faces, and safe havens. They're the people most eager to give you an outlet for everything you're trying to hold inside. Let them help. You'll be happy you did.

Ten Questions: My Compadre Greg

What were the biggest mistakes you made with your kids during your split, and how have you addressed them?
I allowed my ex to dictate certain kids' activities on my nights with them. I should have nipped that in the bud and not allowed her to schedule anything on my days unless I agreed to it. I also realized, only about a year ago, that these are the best years with my kids (they're now eight and ten), and they're fleeting. I know there will be a time when they won't talk to me as much, won't sleep in my bed, won't hug me. I'd been in the habit of, once I got them home from school, letting them chill, watch TV, or use electronics while I

caught up with work. When I would take them on holidays, I'd relax instead of making the effort to play with them in the water or on the sand. In the city, we'd go to movies or for dinner, or engage in other programmed activities.

Then I told myself that for the kids to feel truly loved and confident, they needed more touching, playing, and quality time. I bought a bunch of board games and a deck of cards. I told my kids that whenever they wanted to play a game, I'd say yes, and I stuck to that promise. Also, at several points each night while they were watching TV or playing on their devices (I still want them to have chill time), I'd yell from my bedroom to one or the other to come to my office and would demand a big hug and two minutes of talk time while they sat on my lap, after which they could return to the TV.

The biggest impact has been from playing tickle games. I started instituting ten to twenty minutes of nightly tickling and invented about eight different tickle games: Crusher, Tornado, Sandwich, and so on. Sometimes I surprise them, sometimes I let them choose. They prefer tickle time to watching TV or playing on electronics. They ask for it. I believe it's tickle time that they'll remember when they get older.

What's been your greatest challenge?

When we first split, my ex and I were on good terms, so the only issue was to explain to my three-year-old why Mommy and Daddy were not living in the same house. My son was six months old, so there was no issue there. My ex and I were being, I feel, awesome co-parents, to the point that we took family vacations, went to dinner and movies together, and so forth. Unfortunately, things then got nasty. She met a guy, and within six months was engaged and bought a house a hundred kilometres away. She decided she wanted me out of the picture and for the new guy to take over as dad. Since, it's been a series of putting out fires and, sometimes, telling the kids hard truths.

My ex chose to put the kids between us. She'd tell them they were moving to another city, doing new activities, getting new friends, they wouldn't see Daddy as much, etc., without telling me.

I would find out via the kids. That stuff continues to happen. Or she'd tell the kids I didn't want them to travel with her, Daddy doesn't want the kids to be happy with a new family, and so on. Navigating all that has been challenging. One tries to take the high road and not get involved in the tit-for-tat. Do you tell the kids lies to protect them, or give them some hard truths? Eventually, I had enough, and decided the best way to deal with things is to play lawyer. If you present evidence in a clear way and ask the children what they think is happening, I find they make the right judgment. Avoiding the topic doesn't work, but presenting your case logically does. Kids make up their own minds eventually.

Can you describe your lowest or hardest moments with your kids?
Once I started to get wind of the stuff my ex was doing — that there was the possibility that she could win a legal battle to relocate the kids a hundred kilometres away, that she would tell the kids stuff without telling me, that she was asking them to call her new fiancé "Papa," I experienced a lot of sleepless nights. People know me as a fighter. But it sucked to feel helpless in the face of the constantly moving target that is family law.

How about moments when you saw light at the end of the tunnel?
There were several. But some were ups preceding another down. Some were pleasant surprises, like my ex proposing a deal to keep the kids in the city for school if we moved their school to the west end. She was worried that if she lost the court case, she'd be screwed as she would not be able to drive the kids to school. There were numerous other wins because my ex is not logical and cannot make up her own mind.

In your view, what do kids need most from their dad during or after a breakup?
They need you to stay cool. They need the sound of reason and explanation. They need a warm tone of voice. And, as I said above, they need quality time with you, which in my case, after I decided to

invest proper time with them, took the form of board games, tennis in the park, hide and seek, and, most important, being tactile. My ex would try to buy their love with trips, gifts, and money. I told myself not to play that game and to be authentic instead, and it was the right decision. They need genuine reassurance of your love.

How much emotion did you show your kids with regard to your split? Where do you stand on how much "real" they should see versus how much they should be protected?
I never let myself lose my cool in front of them. If your kids keep seeing you getting upset, they may resist sharing information. My kids are open with me and report on what goes on in my ex's house. I just nod and listen.

What would you say are the key hurdles to get over as a family before kids can start adjusting to the new normal?
I think the most important thing is that both parents sit together, literally physically together, to explain things to the kids, if not right at the outset, then at least after things have had a chance to settle. It tells the kids that the parents are on the same page (even if they're not) and that they're not fighting (even if they are). It also gives the kids assurance that it isn't their fault, confidence to move forward, and creates less chance of their playing one parent against the other.

How do you handle the practical issues of two households?
Things were harmonious for a while. Then my ex moved far away and the custody fight began. Because of the distance between households, there is plenty of conflict regarding the weekly schedule. For example, my ex signs the kids up for activities closer to her home, preventing me from, for instance, being able to get to my son's football games. She does this deliberately. Co-parenting works best when both parents agree on the extracurricular programs, and the schedule for taking the kids to and from. Because of this unnecessary complexity, my son misses half of his games. My daughter was in Mandarin classes on Saturday mornings for years. Her Mandarin was

getting good, but because it was too far from my ex's, she refused to take her to the classes. In the last year, my daughter's Mandarin has all but evaporated.

What are your top three pieces of advice to other dads for maintaining a loving and healthy relationship with their kids after a split?
One, do everything you can to stay calm. Your kids need to feel they can share with someone. If both parents are angry, they won't share with either of you.

Two, be tactile. Give them lots of hugs. Physical contact is important.

Three, make sure you engage in quality time, even if it's in small doses. Doing something together every day, like tennis, wrestling, or even watching TV with your arm around your kid, is important.

And here's another one: ask lots of questions. Kids often don't share difficult emotions or issues, but if you ask the right questions, they will open up.

9

Harnessing Your Libido

I admit, I have a tremendous sex drive. My boyfriend lives forty miles away.

— PHYLLIS DILLER

You are a vital guy, with lots to give and share. Your engine is still running as hot as it was when you were a teenager. And, despite the practical and emotional hardship of all other parts of your split, you feel, let's be honest, newly liberated as a man. At the same time, you're aware that your kids aren't exactly going to be cheering from the stands as you meet new people and explore new possibilities. Still, you want to be (mostly) honest and help them understand that Daddy is a person too, with normal human needs and ... on the other hand, maybe not.

Let's face it: sometimes you feel like you're oversharing, because you want to stay close to your kids. At other times you feel you're hiding too much, because you aren't really sure what they can or cannot handle. What's the right balance between respecting your kids' age and stage, and helping them get used to the new circumstances? How much about a new relationship should you share, and how much should you keep off their radar? Should you be upfront with them about the new people who may enter your life? Should you wait until you become potentially serious about someone before you introduce them into your kids' lives? Should you tell sons certain things and shelter daughters? Or maybe the reverse? Should your teen be privy to certain information that your primary-schooler shouldn't? Does it depend on the child? Perhaps you're asking yourself these same questions.

Maybe, you think sometimes, you should just shut it down and never date again, so you don't have to deal with any of this. Your brain is telling you the monastery looks pretty good right now, while your body is saying, *The hell with that, let's get out there!* So again, what's the right approach? Ease into new relationships? Put yourself on the sidelines for a while so you can focus on the practical and emotional family matters at hand, then dive into the dating game headfirst? Not look for opportunities, but not pass them up?

There are lots of questions surrounding the new you and the natural desires you have. In this chapter, I'd like to talk about how to direct that energy in ways that make sense, how and when to talk to your kids about your love life, and why, over time, all they really need to know is that, regardless of who else may come into the picture, you love them more than anyone else, just as you did before.

I don't know how much sex you were or weren't having in your married relationship, but I do know that even in good marriages, sex on average is not exactly happening around the clock. And if your relationship was going downhill, chances are there wasn't a lot of sex happening, except maybe distraction sex, or going-through-the-motions sex, or frustrated sex. So now you may be feeling like a stallion let loose from the stable, or a tiger on the prowl, but you don't know where to prowl to find … um, another tiger. Tigress. Sorry, let me try that again. You may feel as though you have a lot of carnal energy, and you're feeling a certain need to … meet new … no, explore the opportunity of…. All right, I'm being evasive. You'd like to connect with a new woman since you haven't been with anyone other than your wife for however number of years. You're a man, you're flesh and blood, and even though you've been going through a hard time, you're excited about the chance to rediscover a side of yourself that may have been tamped down lately.

That isn't to say sexual yearning is your primary driver right now. The practical and emotional ordeal of a separation can drain a man of anything other than the desire to lie down and sleep. That may be your current state. But at some point, the resurgence is going to happen. You'll know when it does. It will feel like a transition from exhaustion, withdrawal, and reluctance to renewed confidence, interest, and curiosity. When it does happen, like the proverbial floodgates opening, you may feel as, um, animated as a teenager reliving puberty, with all the same hankering but thankfully without the acne and cracking voice. That reawakening may occur as the discovery of a warm connection and innate closeness, or physical attraction and heady chemistry. Or both. In Fulvia, I was fortunate enough to find someone who fulfills both needs: a person with whom I felt a deep, instinctive bond and who at the same time made me insatiable with desire.

Billy Crystal has a bit from his early stand-up days that cracks me up every time I watch it. He talks about the first onslaught of raging pubescent desire. "Sexually, I was nuts," he says. "Around fifteen, you get that voice. You get that little moustache, where you look like half the women in Newark. And my glands were yelling at me. I was uncontrollable. I was

---

A Few Words from My Buddy Brad

I went through a tough split about five years before meeting my current wife. I found it helpful to know I wasn't alone, or, that is, didn't have to be. It's important, when you're feeling that way, to be aware of the presence and support of others. Rationally, I knew the passage would at some point end. Irrationally, I was not as confident about it as I would like to have been. That ongoing reassurance from others helped a lot. Also, upon reflection, returning to the "market" as soon as I was able to helped. Having other women show interest (and display the physical manifestation of that interest — ahem) was an important and helpful part of the passage. It helped me re-find me.

like a Geiger counter for skirts." He does a side-splitting imitation of his penis obsessively directing him toward anything that moves, accompanied by a low stentorian voice repeating, "Now, now, now."

That may be something like the way you feel at present. And if it is, you may be thinking, *Where do I go? What do I do? What are the current rules? How am I supposed to conduct myself? What's changed? What hasn't?* The great news is that there are more ways than ever to meet people today — the traditional club scene if that's your thing, online dating if it appeals to you (many people meet that way), participating in community groups or associations, joining a gym, accepting friends' invitations to parties and dinners, hell, just going to the grocery store, bookstore, or mall. Be bold and spontaneous, strike up conversations, introduce yourself (in a nice, non-stalker kind of way). There's no predicting where or when you might meet someone with whom you find a mutual spark.

Another advantage of your current situation is that the women you're likely to meet, at least the ones who are part of your peer group, have similar experiences and journeys to yours and are thus, like you, probably more confident about who they are, what they want, and what they will or will not accept. You'll probably find they're more direct, more open, less prone to game playing, more in touch with themselves and their womanhood, and more plainspoken. This generally translates to less anxiety and awkwardness, no matter what phase of the relationship you're in.

In terms of how to approach dating, regardless of when you left the game or returned to it, I can assure you that, fundamentally, not much has changed; insofar as the way people connect is, at its core, the same as it's always been, and still dependent on that mysterious thing called chemistry that no one can define or predict. The means and the settings, of course, change somewhat, but the principles don't. Be nice, be confident but not arrogant, try to be witty and cool, but ultimately be yourself. Don't be overly weird. Pay attention to your appearance, and ask questions about the other person as opposed to talking endlessly about yourself. That same advice would have been applicable five, ten, or fifty years ago.

You'll enjoy discovering the new dating scene, some of which is new and much of which is the same (charming is still charming, creepy is still creepy). You'll probably need a few pointers about what women like and what they are looking for. As a public service to all genders, I went directly to the source — women — by writing an article for a men's magazine recently to find out what was truly important to them, as opposed to what men may assume. I sent a hundred women of various ages fifteen multiple-choice questions about their preferences regarding dating. Here are the fifteen questions, with the top answer shown for each, plus a representative comment.

1. What's your preferred body type?
   a) Bodybuilder
   b) Lean and toned
   c) Boyish
   d) Solid and hefty

   Top answer: Lean and toned is the most popular pick, at 73 percent. You won't find most women drooling over the guy with the huge beer gut, but you also aren't likely to find them fawning over the dude who's built like an air mattress. If you find yourself entering Mr. Olympia territory, you may want to lower the weight and increase the reps.
   Telling comment: "A little size is a plus, but I don't want to walk around with an enormous muscleman."

2. What's your favourite look on a guy?
   a) Three-piece suit
   b) Jeans and T-shirt
   c) Khakis and button-down
   d) Sweats

   Top answer: Forty percent say jeans and tee rule the day. In other words, sloppy is only okay for watching the game with your buddies, and suits are nice for work and formal affairs. Otherwise, stylish and clean — and, most importantly, current — are what count.
   Telling comment: "Conservative can be so hot!"

3. Guys should spend more time on their:
   a) Chest
   b) Hands
   c) Hair
   d) Clothes

Top answer: The clothes have it, to the tune of 68 percent. If a woman can't get past the clothes, it won't matter how good you look underneath. Don't be a lesser dresser.
Telling comment: "Well-dressed men can get away with a lot."

4. On a date, how good do you want the guy to look?
   a) As good as you
   b) Better than you
   c) Worse than you
   d) Doesn't matter, as long as he looks stylish

Top answer: No need to stress — 53 percent of women say it doesn't matter what you're wearing, as long as you pay some attention to how you present yourself. Next time you're about to hop in the car, spend another minute or two in front of the mirror to make sure everything is where it's supposed to be.
Telling comment: "It's a turn-on when the guy you're with cares about his appearance."

5. At which store would you prefer a guy to shop?
   a) Gap
   b) Club Monaco
   c) Abercrombie & Fitch
   d) Armani

Top answer: Club Monaco (35 percent) just edges out the Gap (30 percent). You don't have to break the bank to display yourself impressively. And don't be shy about asking the saleswomen for help.

Telling comment: "I want him to look good, but not like he's trying too hard."

6. Which of the following impresses you the least?
    a) Huge pecs and biceps
    b) Tree-trunk legs
    c) Six-pack abs
    d) Rock-hard glutes

Top answer: Sorry, guys — freaky legs freak her out (65 percent), and massive pecs and guns (32 percent) aren't likely to move the needle much either. Fit and strong is good; busting at the seams is not. (See question 1.)
Telling comment: "I find really muscular guys unimpressive. It's a strong indicator of how they spend their time, and I don't want to be with someone who spends his life at the gym."

7. How do you like your sex?
    a) Long and steamy
    b) Quick and dirty
    c) Full of surprises
    d) Doesn't matter, as long as you get me where I'm going

Top answer: Make like a magician — surprises are the way to go (53 percent). Showing a little imagination doesn't mean you need to install a sex swing; it just means doing more than going through the motions.
Telling comment: "I find it extremely sexy when a guy is so attracted to me that he wants to show me something special."

8. For a first date, you prefer:
    a) Dinner and a movie
    b) A picnic
    c) An amusement park
    d) A baseball or basketball game

Top answer: No need to get fancy — 45 percent of respondents said dinner and a movie still works just as well as ever as a foundational interaction.

Telling comment: "Dinner and a movie may not sound very original, but the dinner means lots of conversation, which is the best way to get to know each other. And the movie is a nice, no-pressure follow-up."

9. At the end of the date, you expect:
   a) A kiss on the cheek
   b) A kiss on the lips
   c) A brief make-out
   d) A polite good night

Top answer: A kiss on the cheek is a safe bet (45 percent), and if you want to plant one on her lips, that's probably okay too (40 percent). A handshake shows indifference, and an open mouth implies arrogance or desperation. Keep it sweet and simple, and think of it as a taste of things to come.

Telling comment: "There's nothing sweeter than a polite kiss to signal affection but not put any pressure on me."

10. Sex will occur:
   a) On the first date, if he's really cool and I'm feeling a bit crazy
   b) By the fourth or fifth date
   c) After a month, no matter how many dates we've been on
   d) Whenever I feel it's right

Top answer: No sense trying to unlock the secret equation — 97 percent of women say they'll let you know when they're ready. Naturally, you'd like a neon sign to flash when the moment is right, but the truth is women decide mostly on instinct and chemistry. So be patient and enjoy it when it comes.

Telling comment: "There's no magic formula for getting

a girl into bed, despite what guys might like to think. The right time is the right time, and we don't know in advance when that's going to be."

11. Flowers are best when:
    a) Given as a form of apology
    b) Given on special occasions
    c) Given once a week
    d) Given for no reason

Top answer: Ninety-five percent of women say a random floral surprise will score you serious points. When you screw up, say you're sorry. On special occasions, buy gifts, go to nice restaurants, write romantic poems. But every now and then, send roses or show up with a fresh-cut bouquet, and when she asks why, say, "Do I need a reason?"
Telling comment: "Knowing you were thought of during the day for no reason puts a smile on your face for the entire week."

12. If a guy wants to have sex with you, he should:
    a) Be willing to flirt for a bit — women like the chase as much as the capture
    b) Bring it up the first time he thinks it
    c) Buy you lots of small gifts
    d) Go base by base, date to date

Top answer: This may not be the answer you're looking for, but 63 percent say the thrill is in the chase. Though of course quite a few men would like to go right from "Hello" to the bedroom, women appreciate the game for its own sake. And which do you prefer, to play the game and get some wins, or sit on the sideline?
Telling comment: "I want you to want me, but not to rush me."

13. The best face is:
    a) Clean-shaven, with no sideburns
    b) Clean-shaven with sideburns
    c) Scruffy
    d) Moustached and bearded

Top answer: Fifty-three percent say clean-cut is the way to go. If a woman is into you, she wants to see your face and kiss it without having to apply burn ointment. Ask yourself whether you prefer women's legs smooth or stubbly. Now think about your face.
Telling comment: "Kissing a guy with facial hair is like rubbing your face on sandpaper."

14. If you could change one thing about all men, you'd make them:
    a) More fashion conscious
    b) Better listeners
    c) More open with their feelings
    d) Less sports obsessed

Top answer: You don't have to give up sports, but do learn to listen (45 percent) and shed the occasional tear (38 percent). Subdue the male urge for logic, reason, and solution seeking. Instead, any time she needs to vent, force yourself to just shut up and listen — and then follow up with by a hug.
Telling comment: "I'd like to make all men better listeners, and at the same time disable whatever switch it is that forces them to give advice."

15. More than anything, a guy can impress you by:
    a) Knowing how to cook
    b) Knowing what buttons to press in bed
    c) Being able to discuss art, politics, and literature
    d) Knowing just the right thing to say to cheer you up

Top answer: Forget acting smart or domestic — just know how to make her smile (73 percent). Being able to handle yourself in the kitchen, the bedroom, and at parties will all earn you kudos, but nowhere near the points you'll get for recognizing when to be serious or sensitive, funny or frank, assertive or accepting.

Telling comment: "How do you know if a guy is the one? He knows what to say, and when to say it."

Every man's emotional state after a breakup is different, because every man's experience leading to that point is different. If you were in a bad relationship in which you didn't feel valued, respected, or desired, then once free you might have the instinct to pursue any woman who comes your way as a way of feeling good again. That's fine. If you and your ex agreed things had just faded away, you might desire an intimate connection with someone who stimulates you and gets the neurons firing. That's also cool. If you were with someone who behaved badly in what you feel are stereotypical ways, you might be turned off women for the moment and disinclined to find out if there are any good ones. Again, perfectly natural.

There are a couple of important things to keep in mind once you do decide to date again. The first is to be careful with regard to your own health. You might feel so liberated that your sense of risk gets subordinated to your sense of lust. Sex always entails risks. Be safe. Be knowledgeable about who you're being intimate with (or considering being intimate with). Be smart in your choices so that you don't end up getting burned for a poor decision in the passion of the moment. (Does it sound like I'm your dad giving you the talk? Sorry. Just trying to look out for you.)

Second is to keep your antennae up when it comes to your kids. Experts differ on the ways to allow your kids exposure to your new life and, potentially, new partners, but they agree resoundingly on one thing: go slowly. While each child is different — each of my three kids reacted in different ways to the idea of my new relationship, from mature acceptance to violent rejection — they are all similar in one way. They need time to adjust.

From an even more practical standpoint, aside from the question of how much or how little to expose your kids to potential dating partners, be careful about what you may accidentally leave around for them to discover. You may find that you thoroughly enjoy the opportunity to flirt, sext, exchange racy pics, or write lewd emails. You may have a library of pictures on your computer in a private file. You may be taking lots of selfies of a particular type to share with those interested. You may be going old school and composing handwritten notes indicating your specific desires to someone with whom you've become enjoyably engaged. You may keep physical articles purchased as part of your newfound freedom in your nightstand.

You see where I'm going. Stumbling upon (or actively looking for, and finding) any of these things could be seriously traumatizing for your kids. They don't like to imagine their parents having sex despite the fact that they must have done so to have created them, never mind being forced to imagine their father with other women. You may feel like a wolf unleashed, but your kids need to know that you're still stable and regular Dad. Go crazy in private. Pursue new things.Enjoy your freedom. Share stories with your buddies. But keep your kids away from the erotic side of your life. In front of them, be the same dad you've always been. Though no doubt happier.

Some Candid Words from My Buddy Tristan

My daughter Chloe had just turned four when my ex and I split. She — Chloe — didn't show any negative signs at first, but she did then become difficult a couple of years later. For example, she started resisting coming to visit me when I arrived at my ex's to pick her up. The main problem I've had is that, with the limited time I have with her, I try to do all the hard work of coaching, disciplining, and providing direction that I feel she doesn't get from her mother. The result is that I'm the bad cop in her life. Fourteen years later, even though her life is a shambles, she won't come live with me because her impression is that, regardless of my behaviour, I'm the father who is always disappointed and giving her grief.

My ex and I talked plenty about how to raise her and were, I thought, on the same page, but the problem is that my ex can't follow her words with commensurate actions, so I end up doing on my own what I thought we'd planned to do in tandem, while she falls back to being the accommodating and easygoing mom, and as a result I look like the asshole. I stopped pressing both my ex and my daughter a couple of years ago and instead just focused on trying to keep it happy and light with Chloe, but she still hides bad news from me because she automatically thinks I'll be angry, even though I haven't responded that way for years now — not to mention it's not anger I think I express, but frustration. But I understand how, when she was young, she wouldn't have been able to tell the difference. With older kids, you'd see the effects more immediately. You'd need to be more supportive than disciplining.

The biggest challenge I've had in staying in Chloe's life was the fact that my ex moved away from me a few months after we split. She was fired from her job because she wasn't going to it. She couldn't afford her apartment, and I didn't want to pay for it on top of child support, plus paying off our shared debt. So I didn't have much choice but to let her move in with her parents, who lived far away. I assumed that once she was back on her feet, she would move back into the city, because she hates the town where her parents live. But she needed them to watch our daughter while she worked, so a few years later she got an apartment in that same town. I would rather she'd have moved back into the city and used me for help watching Chloe after school, but, despite having joint custody, there wasn't much I could do.

I know of families in which the spouses live close to each other and the kids live in the different houses on alternating weeks and travel to their school from each location, which sounds like the best kind of setup, though I have no empirical knowledge on how well it works. The biggest issue one needs to look out for, which was the problem for me and others I've seen, is any sizable gap between you and your ex in attitudes, behaviours, or lifestyles. Big differences in this regard mean the kids might naturally start to favour one life over the other, and the losing spouse in that scenario obviously stands to suffer a lot. I know of one two-child family in which each child lives permanently with each parent because that's what they've stated is their preference.

So things can go in a number of different directions, and, to be honest, you'll likely have less influence over this than you'd like, since you can't control your ex. In the end, there are only two things you can control: yourself, and your relationship with your kids.

10

Nurturing Your Heart

Keep love in your heart. A life without it is like a sunless garden
when the flowers are dead.

— OSCAR WILDE

Maybe you were with your partner for a few decades, maybe a few years. Either way, you've evolved in your own skin. You're a different person, emotionally, psychologically, and spiritually. You have a better idea, now, of what you really want, because you're older and wiser, and you've learned a lot about the things you like and dislike, and the way you want to experience love, romance, and intimacy. As a partner, you've come to better understand the habits and behaviours you tend to default to, your blind spots and biases, the way you express affection and passion, your ways of coping with stress, managing tough moments, and having difficult conversations, and the instances in which you shine versus the ones where you could improve.

And as a man, you grasp more clearly what you want in a relation-ship — you're more willing to speak up for what matters to you, are less willing to make unfair compromises, you know what count for you as small things or deal breakers, and you appreciate the points of connection and compatibility that make a relationship truly sing. More importantly, even though your split may feel negative on the whole, one undeniable positive coming from it is the learning you did in that relationship that you can bring to the next, which benefits you as well as whoever you find. Out of the depths of your sadness and pain comes a capacity to be a richer you, a man of new strength and vulnerability, and a father of new wisdom and understanding.

This evolution creates a new opportunity: the opportunity to find someone who can make you feel brand new, a reborn, fuller version of yourself. From the torture of your current transition comes the wonderful chance to give and receive love in ways you never imagined, be appreciated in ways you never expected, experience closeness in ways you never knew existed, and feel parts of you open up that you never knew were there. Let's talk about the ongoing matter of your heart, the elusive definition of happiness we all seek, and the reasons you still deserve to find it.

———————

Men love to love. We love romance. We love intimacy. But after a breakup — even a "good" breakup — you may sense that, while your body feels open for business, your heart is temporarily off limits. This may come in the form of a simultaneous discovery that you genuinely like a particular woman and also feel oddly fearful, or even angry, about it. There are a few reasons for this:

- **Self-protection.** Your heart and soul have been wounded. You're not in a rush to put yourself in a potentially exposed position again. The easiest way to prevent this is for you not to open yourself up. So while your loins may be saying, "Let's *go!!!*" your heart may be saying, "I think I'll sit this one out."
- **Emotional fatigue.** Whether you were in a relationship for six months or two decades, your heart was "on" all the time. It was invested. It absorbed all the different emotions that go with a relationship, all the highs and lows, the

simplicities and complexities. You might feel the desire to give it a well-deserved break. Your heart has put in a lot of service time. You aren't decommissioning it, but maybe you just want to give it a vacation.

- **Your kids**. One of the men I interviewed for this book explained his feelings clearly: "I feel like I have a good heart and look forward to being able to share it with someone again. But right now, it belongs just to my kids. I don't know when I'll be ready to open it back up to others. I just know it's not now." On dates he would be totally honest with the woman he was with, telling her he was testing whether he could be present and open with others yet, but that he really didn't know. He would apologize in advance, giving potential partners an out. Sometimes they took it. Sometimes one date turned into a few, and they would see a movie, go for ice cream, talk, but ultimately he would apologize, saying he just wasn't there. Once or twice the dating led to sex, but he was going through it without really being present. He knew it, and so did those he was with.

These feelings, and numerous others, are natural barriers to the instinct to want to offer up your heart again. A family breakup, for an indeterminate period, devastates everyone involved in it. You will need time to put yourself back together before your heart is ready to be shared with someone else.

You may also need some time to get reacquainted with yourself. You've spent a major period of your life defined, at least partially, by the relationship you were in, and the person with whom you were in it. You're now entering a new stage, one in which — for the first time in a while, maybe a long while — you'll be defined by your own self and by your kids. This shift by itself takes a lot of time and energy, including, as family therapist Dr. Rotem Regev suggests, different introspective questions you may find yourself seeking to answer — who you are, what you want, where your priorities lie. Those priorities, at least for now, are your kids and little else.

"Many dads experience a new-found curiosity about their identity," Dr. Regev advises. "The questions 'Who am I?' and 'What do I want to do with the rest of my life?' come to the forefront. Questions about re-coupling, readiness for it, the merit in it, arise. But often I hear separated dads say things like, 'I'm there sitting at a bar, the world is my oyster, but all I want to do is coach my daughter's soccer team.'" (I talk more about your new identity as a single dad in Chapter 12.)

This mode of thinking makes perfect sense. Given the torment you've been through and the fact that you don't know when it may end, simple probably looks very attractive right now. The more burned you feel, the more cynical you might be. The more cynical you are, the more you may feel that relationships are not viable. Perhaps you've come to believe genuine compatibility is a foolish concept and you might as well just try to have sex with different people with no investment or commitment while focusing on your kids and playing sports with your buddies. All of which mean easy relationships with no complications. Such thoughts are a natural outcome of your feelings of hurt and self-protection. You were in a relationship that wasn't meant to end, but it did. When it comes to your heart, you could be questioning not only the validity of committed relationships, but also your ability to be in one. You might be feeling skeptical about everything from the sanctity of a monogamous relationship to putting the time and energy into being with someone again.

Perhaps you're fearful of the unpredictability of things, given how your own relationship went compared to the vision you had for it. You chose someone who you believed was a match for you, and that person turned out to be so not a match that you had to break up. It stands to reason that you might not exactly be Cupid's biggest endorser. Maybe at this point your attitude is more like "The best I can do is hope to mostly like someone and have them mostly like me, and overlook the stuff that drives us nuts about each other." Maybe you feel as if you can't even trust your own ability to decide who might be good for you and who might not be, since you already messed up that decision once, badly enough that your kids have to suffer for it.

Could I ask you a favour? Give yourself a break. And give yourself time. Your heart has been darkened, and it needs time to become light again. You are pouring every ounce of care and devotion into your kids' well-being, and every bit of your intelligence and resilience into the practical issues demanding resolution. Try not to be frustrated with yourself if you don't quite feel like there's much of you, if any, to be shared just now. When I asked other dads about the subject of post-split romance and relationships, I heard two things again and again: don't rush; and don't give up. I agree with both notions.

I also believe in something I call Year Zero. You'll hear a lot of people tell you it takes at least a year, possibly two, for you and your family to get back to anything resembling normal. Based on my own experience and the experiences of so many others I've talked to, I actually consider the first year after a split Year Zero, since that year is typically characterized less by progress than by mere survival. Many men who have endured splits told me to brace myself for at least a year of insanity and hell before any kind of settling would occur. They were as right as right can be. That first year was more like trying to walk through a deep murk, holding my kids' hands and promising them the clouds would lift even though I had no evidence that they would.

During Year Zero, emotions aren't close to settling down yet, because they're usually still escalating. In that same period, practical matters aren't yet getting sorted out; they're just starting to be discussed. To expect any level of growth or degree of ease in this period is, in most cases, unfair. Unfair to yourself. The moment of the split is your own personal Big Bang. And just as the universe stayed dark for hundreds of millions of years before light emerged, you, too, need time to progress from that initial blast to a calmer state.

"One thing we can definitely say is that the process almost always takes longer than you think," says author Alyson Schafer. "While rebounding from the stress of the decision you've made, there is an initial period where there are just so many things to be figured out, and you're carrying so much tension around. It is a massive readjustment. It could be two years just for the fog to lift, much less for you to be in a position where you can enter into a new relationship." She suggests giving yourself time not only to sort through all the immediate family matters, but also for introspection and reflection about the new phase you're entering and the person you want to be as you embark on it.

"This is a reinvention," she says. "Before starting to share with someone else, a lot of dads ought to first think about the question, 'Who do I want to be? How do I want this new version of my life, and myself, to look?' That doesn't happen quickly, given all the practical things that need to be prioritized. Your first concern needs to be your kids, and your being a healthy adult. Only then can you start to put some thought into yourself and what this next chapter means. Slow and steady wins the race."

However, as numerous experts have noted, many dads go the other route and fling themselves into a relationship with the first woman who gives them attention following the split, or, in some cases, anyone who is a contrast to their ex. Psychologist Andrew Shaul remarks that one of the most common mistakes he sees dads making after a split is plunging whole hog into new relationships before allowing themselves the proper time to heal. "I see so many fathers dive into another relationship, where I feel it would benefit them to be more patient," he says.

You need to allow your heart to regain its structural integrity, figuratively speaking. It's a good heart, but it's been damaged. So why might you want to jump hastily into another relationship if your heart has been battered and your emotional armour cracked? For exactly that reason. You want to protest against the pain, and, maybe, the creeping thought of having failed or been rejected. "There may be a certain level of fear and desperation," says Shaul, "and with it [comes] the desire to say, 'I'm a good guy, I'm interesting, I'm desirable.'" This self-validation logic, he suggests, is straightforward, even if it may be skewed. "The relationship failed, my wife doesn't want to be with me, and that affects my self-esteem, so I want to feel good about myself, and what's the best way to do that? Find someone who's into me, somebody who isn't my wife or like my wife, so I can say, *Look, I'm proving to myself, and maybe to my kids, that I'm not the problem here.*"

But when dads fall into new relationships based on these factors — desperation, anger, the desire to prove they're worthy of attention — the common result is a level of fulfillment or satisfaction inverse to the speed with which those relationships started. These relationships tend to lack the chance to provide true pleasure or contentment because the person entering into it has not truly opened back up. "I've found a lot of times fathers feel excited about the independence and freedom they now have to do what they want, try things they've never tried," says Shaul, "but at the same time they find themselves very lonely. This is natural. It takes time. Take a period to get comfortable with yourself. Let the dust settle."

Shaul describes this process as *re-grounding*, an apt term. The anguish and intensity you feel as a result of the family breakup is akin to having your spirit blown to smithereens. Your heart has to settle back into an intact state — except that part happens in super slo-mo. While that re-grounding process is occurring, you are, in a sense, in limbo, insofar as the pieces are still floating and regathering. So you're neither your old self, which is permanently gone, nor your new self, which is still forming. And if you yourself aren't whole again, you probably aren't well disposed to connect with someone else in any substantial way. "Allow the process of coming back into yourself before trying to share that self with another," advises Shaul. "We make better decisions from a position of balance. We don't make our best decisions when our driving emotions are guilt, shame, anger, or loneliness."

I refer again to the Big Bang analogy. With all that dark matter pervading your internal universe, and all those elements violently whizzing around within it, you can hardly operate from a place of calm and clarity. You're containing a world of volatility inside that hasn't yet settled. But when light starts to emerge, you can see better, and when the elements start to resolve, amazing things can begin to grow.

———————

Actor Loretta Young said, "Love isn't something you find. Love is something that finds you." You might encounter someone for whom you come to feel true affection a week after splitting, or six months, or five years. That affection might turn into a glow filling your entire soul, or it might not. It's not possible to tell from the start. It's also not possible to say how fast or how slowly you may find someone. This isn't within your control. When I met Fulvia, I knew right away that my heart had changed forever. I hadn't asked to meet her then. That was simply when she appeared. The timing was unpredictable; the feeling, irrefutable.

Don't be surprised if a new relationship happens when you're least expecting it to, or begins in the least likely way. My meeting Fulvia occurred due to the convergence of an unlikely set of circumstances. I'd agreed to co-write a new book with the husband of a childhood friend. This required me to travel from Canada to France to take the course on which the book would be based, at the business school where the friend's husband was an instructor. Fulvia, living in Italy, was at a personal and professional crossroads. She had chosen to take the same course at the same time, partly for career reasons, partly because her gut told her to. There she appeared, and there I fell. I felt light and happy in her presence; I wanted her to know everything about me, and I wanted to know everything about her in return. I was elated at the experience of talking to her; she produced an unyielding inferno inside me; and, most importantly, she made me want to open my heart.

You might experience an instant shock of harmony or a gradual meeting of the minds. You might feel tentative about opening yourself emotionally for a long period, or, like me, you might meet someone whom you know your heart was meant for all along. Either way, the eventual re-blooming of your spirit, and the feeling of someone else showing it care and tenderness, will be wonderful. You'll have gone through an arduous journey to reach a new stage and a new you. As part of this transformation, your experience of love, amorousness, and synchronicity can be redefined and transcended.

This new feeling of connection, and with it a renewed faith in romance, may be accompanied by an eagerness to let your kids know about the new person who is making you feel so good inside, and so happy in many new and different ways. Of course, there's an inherent conflict here. First, as I've said before, kids want their lives to be predictable and familiar, and that condition has been shattered by their parents breaking up. Second, even kids who understand the reason for their parents having split will still always harbour a secret desire for them to get back together. Finally, and most importantly, kids are focused on themselves because they're kids, so even though they want you to be happy, their main frame of reference is their world, not yours. Ultimately, they'll be happier and feel better to see you happier and better. But that won't happen overnight. The family breakup has blown apart the tidy order of their existence. Your bringing someone new into their lives requires another big adjustment.

Most experts agree on two key guidelines when it comes to introducing someone new into your kids' lives. The first: take it slow. Don't force a new partner onto them, or them onto a new partner. Doing so will only impede the opportunities for both to get to know each other in an easy and real way. Remember that when children are told Mommy and Daddy are breaking up, it is the unknowns that terrify them. They've always lived with both parents; now they don't know if both will continue to be there. Show them that your devotion to them remains complete and permanent, minimizing the potential for them to feel threatened by someone new stealing your affection, attention, and time.

The second guideline: make the introduction of a new partner low-key, and do it with minimal pressure. When you do bring that someone new into the mix, maximize the fun while minimizing the drama. Though it is, of course, a big deal, try not to make it seem like one. Do something casual together, like going to a park or seeing a movie. In other words, when introducing your new partner, don't make it *about* introducing your new partner.

As with every other aspect of the split and the stages proceeding from it, try to see this change through your kids' eyes. If you focus on the introduction of someone new, this can inadvertently make your kids feel secondary in importance. So, when you do introduce them, try to let your kids feel that you're doing something normal with them and the new person is being integrated into it — as opposed to your kids being integrated into your new relationship.

I started this chapter with a quote from Oscar Wilde comparing love to a garden. I'd like to conclude it with another quote, from Khalil Gibran: "If your heart is a volcano, how shall you expect flowers to bloom?" Oscar

Wilde was an Irish poet and playwright; Khalil Gibran, a Lebanese artist and writer. Isn't it fascinating that these two men from different periods and places portrayed love in so similar a manner? There is something special in the metaphor they use. Flowers can be damaged, gardens compromised. But with the right conditions, the soil becomes rich again, and the flowers bloom.

My Friend Ryan

The following story sent to me by my friend Ryan illustrates how the end of a marriage can lead to a fresh start.

> During the six years I was with my ex, my life went on a steady downward trend. I was fired from two jobs because my focus wasn't on my work, we were in large debt, I had no friends left and no social life, and by the end, life in our apartment was unbearable. (Even our cats were unhappy. I'm serious.)
>
> When I left my wife, I moved in with my mom. Five months later, I was promoted to my first management position. A year later, I met Julia. Two years after that, she and I were engaged and I paid off the last of my debt. Four months later, we bought a house, and soon after, I was promoted again. I also completed a university degree part-time. Today I enjoy a strong reputation at work, am financially secure, and have a deliriously happy marriage.
>
> Leaving was a huge moment for me. When I turned thirty, I looked at my life and realized I had sleepwalked through it. I had succeeded at most things without much effort and just went with the flow. That's one of the reasons I ended up in an ill-advised marriage. It's no coincidence that I left

one month after turning thirty. It was a true reckoning for me about what I'd done with the years before, and what I wanted to do with the ones after. From the moment I left, I began to take ownership of my life. Any success and good fortune I've had since is attributable to that turning point. Of course, I wish I'd had this awakening ten years before, and sometimes wonder how much further I'd be if I'd gotten my shit together earlier, but there's no sense in wasting time and energy lamenting that. I can only deal with what's in front of me.

My family told me I'd turned into a different person during my marriage, and that quickly after, I turned back into my old self. The best thing I got from going through a bad marriage was an enormous amount of learning. It's no fluke that my new wife and I are so good together. I know now what I need in life and am not hesitant about making changes when something is too negative or compromises the things that bring positives. It sounds so simple. But it took a long time to get here.

Ryan's story is a common one, which I have heard in endless variation from men who were in relationships that somehow constrained, instead of enhanced, who they were. The reasons they felt this restriction are irrelevant. As I said, the purpose of this book is not to say "You were good and your ex was bad." There are two people in every relationship. The purpose is to talk about who you are becoming today, and how to celebrate that guy.

The most common element of stories like Ryan's was that the dads struggling through them felt they were not able to have the relationship they would have liked with their kids because they weren't free to be themselves. Despite the ordeal of your family breakup, one priceless gift is certain to emerge. You will find a new freedom in being yourself, and your kids will be the most important beneficiaries.

11

Adapting Your Outlook

Of all the things that take a hit during a family breakup, your general philosophy or perspective might be among the biggest. You are the same person, but your existence as you know it has been dealt a massive blow, and the fallout can make you wake up on many days wondering how a life that seemed so pleasantly ordinary has become so unhinged. Most of the time, you might find yourself battling a general sense of confusion and helplessness where solidity and certainty existed before. You might find yourself experiencing some *woe-is-me* moments, small pockets of misery you try to reject but which come anyway. These kinds of moments might feel foreign to you, because (a) you've had a pretty decent life so far; (b) your parents taught you never to feel sorry for yourself; (c) you've never faced a problem you didn't feel you could soldier through; or (d) all of the above.

You may not like how strange these moments feel, or how often they surge forth. Guess what: it's okay that you're having them, because you aren't exactly supposed to be doing cartwheels right now. (I remember one therapy session I did with my ex in which she was telling the therapist I was acting strange because of how sad I was. The therapist replied, "You're going through something extraordinarily hard. What would be strange is if he were acting normal.") On many days, you're experiencing something that feels nearly unendurable. You'll come out the other side okay, thanks to that ultimate healer, time. But while time does its work, you need to be able to manage the stuff in between, and that stuff includes the attitude you take into each day.

———————

I found one of the most difficult things about my split to be an existential conflict. Due to whatever mix of ingredients produced me, I've always been a happy person. I always woke up optimistic and eager about the day. I always had a light attitude toward any circumstance or situation. Now, suddenly, apart from when I was with, or at least speaking to, my kids or Fulvia, I was sad. My sadness was profoundly deep. I wanted to get happy, but I couldn't. I faked it at work and everywhere else. No matter how bad I felt, I made a promise to myself not to let it change the way I treated others. But every smile I gave, artificial as it was, involved a huge effort. The only moments of joy I derived were from, as I said, contact with my kids, who lit me up just by being themselves, or seeing Fulvia, who had opened an entire world of new feelings for me, all of them blissful.

Being dominated by gloom like this disturbed me deeply. When I'd experienced darkness before, it had been the exception. Now lightness had become the exception. I didn't know whether I had changed forever, if I would be this sad person for the rest of my life. I felt a strange and draining ongoing internal scuffle between my normal positive disposition, which was wanting to get to the surface, and the daily avalanche of sorrow keeping it down. Worse, I'd made my kids sad. So I had to ask myself some awful questions: *Have I permanently stolen their happiness? And is there a bigger crime a parent can commit?*

For Cory's birthday seven months after my split, he asked to go on a hike with a group of buddies to his favourite place, a natural spot by Lake Ontario with rocks and water and forest and cliffs. Except he didn't want me to come. My ex and I talked about it and decided I should go, both for safety and also for the more complicated unspoken statement that I was going to be there even when my son said he didn't want me to be. Neither of us had any idea if this was the right decision, but that's what we agreed on.

During the first part of the hike, I wanted to annihilate myself. While Cory's friends whooped and hollered, roaming and adventuring and playing tag in the high grass, Cory drifted around looking lost, expressionless, chin down, barely interacting with his friends, sadness visible all over his body. His behaviour tore my heart to shreds. I tried to shake myself out of this feeling. I wondered whether my sadness was being reflected in his. After a while either I broke out of it, or he did, or we both did, but at some point I saw his body kind of wake back up and he became himself again, hiking along the cliffs and through the rugged forest, wrestling and laughing with his buddies, commenting on the views and the scenery, and tiring himself out with the general rambunctiousness and mischief-making of boys.

As I've repeated a few times, no part of the overall transition through a family breakup is linear or isolated from any other part, so I don't want to make it seem as though he, or I, went from one unqualified state to another. The process goes in loops and cycles, which often feel random. The following week I was back to feeling overpoweringly sad. When I dropped Cory off at school, I'd watch with deep self-loathing as he walked away from the car with his head down, projecting a total absence of energy or cheer. I'd have instantly accepted misery for the rest of my life in exchange for his being happy for one day.

But again, it takes time. Unfortunately, much more than we'd like. I wanted to press an invisible button and switch everyone's mood back to where it was at some indeterminate point in the past. However, that was out of my control. The only things within my control were the love I could show my kids, the consistency and presence I could give them, and the battle I could continue to wage against my own anguish.

Things changed, ever so slowly. The following year's birthday party for Cory was at a parkour gym. I took him and his buddies, with no argument from him, and no insistence that my ex be there in addition to, or instead of, me. He and his friends enjoyed themselves and ate enough pizza afterward to punish my wallet, which made me smile. Most importantly, he was full of vigour and merriment, and I guess I was too.

The year after that, we celebrated his birthday at a treetop climbing place in a forest north of the city. This time my ex and I took Cory and his friends together, along with Dustin and Alisha, and it was a memorably great day, full of fun and laughs. It was the kind of day I'd hoped might be possible at some point, representing passage into a new phase in which we could still exist as a family in certain moments and contexts, and have those moments be ones of brightness and positivity instead of heaviness and tension. Along we went, and, with time, harmonious moments slowly started to become more frequent than frictional ones.

Not to belabour the point, but when I say slowly, I mean *slowly*. Your happiness is obviously tied to that of your kids (or, as many have put it, "You're only as happy as your least happy child"), and your ability to make the transition to a happier place will be aligned with theirs. Your disposition on any given day will be to some degree a mirror of whatever they are feeling, and expressing. On some days, you will be unavoidably sad together. On others, happy moments occur. These happy moments are tiny cracks in the armour, and eventually enough of them will occur, in close enough proximity, that the armour will break apart, and you will have discovered that you are at a good place, characterized by light and exuberance, just like before. Maybe even a better place.

Honesty alert: though we are much further down the road as a family, and things are far better than they were, and we've established a rhythm of sorts, and my kids all seem to be doing well, I still get sad. I have not gotten used to not seeing my children every day. A couple of people told me I would get used to it. I won't. I am able to handle it when, for example, they go to overnight camp, because that is a positive experience we have actively given them and that I know they love. But I have not gotten any better at managing my internal state on the normal days when I don't see them, because it is a negative, saddening experience they had no choice in making. When I don't see them, I feel somewhat empty. When I see them again, I fill back up. The cycle goes on. I just want to be honest.

But — and this is big — my time with them is pure joy. Due to the combination of belief in having made the right decision, forward movement into the new life chapter, and a beautiful partner who gives me constant love, support, and understanding, I am myself again. And my kids, in response, are their true selves with me. We are joyous and natural and us. We sing, play, argue, act silly, cook, invent. Even when they misbehave individually or antagonize each other, I love it, because they are being their normal selves, and I am my normal self in return. I'm delighted to get up early to make their lunches. I'm utterly content to sit on the couch with them and cuddle together in front of a movie. I'm overcome with happiness when I tuck them in at night.

My friend Arjun captures this dichotomy expertly. "When my mom had a minor heart attack years ago, the doctor explained that a small part of her heart had died, and the tissue wouldn't work anymore, but that enough of the organ was still healthy that she could continue on. I view my divorce as a similar situation. It left a scar, it still causes me pain, but I was able to move on." I agree with this strongly, and I don't find it a pessimistic view — rather, the opposite. From the most difficult trials we emerge stronger and better, though we still necessarily carry forward the pain and challenge of the experience that led us there. In the words of author Jodi Picoult, "The human capacity for burden is like bamboo — far more flexible than you'd ever believe at first glance." I once heard someone describe resilience as being like "a million rubber bands." It's true: you keep bouncing back, partly because you have to for your kids, partly because the alternative is resigning yourself to melancholy, and we all prefer to seek happiness than accept despair.

Still, no matter what type of personality you have or how hardy you typically are, the passage through a family split can grind you down. It's no surprise if you're feeling beat up on certain days, and maybe a little helpless, or hopeless, or both. On those days, it's nice when even a sliver of light can make it through the gloom. Here are some simple things you can do to help. They won't write the separation agreement any faster, put money in your pocket, or provide you more hours of sleep, but they may allow you to breathe a bit easier for that minute, or hour, or day.

- **Read.** Not just books like this. Read fiction. Read biographies. Read memoirs. Reading provides a pleasant

escape, and it keeps you stimulated, or maybe just inno-
cently distracted. Your life for a while is going to be heavy
and complicated. Reading helps lighten the mind and can
make things feel simple for a while.

- **Read poetry**. I recommend Wordsworth, Shelley,
  Browning, Frost, Emily Dickinson, e e cummings, Robert
  William Service, and, though I know he's more famous for
  the suspense and horror stories, Edgar Allan Poe. Try the
  poems "Casey at the Bat," by Ernest Lawrence Thayer, and
  "In Flanders Fields," by John McCrae, plus one called "Mrs.
  Malone," by Eleanor Farjeon, which my kids love me to
  read to them because they know I won't make it to the end
  without starting to weep, which amuses them greatly.
- **Look at pictures of baby animals of any species.** I'm
  serious. Search a random picture of a baby elephant, zebra,
  bear, or rhino. You'll find it hard to stay blue.
- **Volunteer or do charity work.** The lower you feel inside,
  the more of a boost you will get when you give of your
  time and energy to others. Again, this won't solve your
  practical situation or improve your external circumstances,
  but it will remind you that others are fighting their battles
  too, many of them harder than yours — and, at a very basic
  human level, it will make you feel good at a time when
  most things are not. Mother Teresa said, "Spread love
  everywhere you go. Let no one ever come to you without
  leaving happier."

When you're really hurting, show your kids you can
still spread cheer. It's a wonderful example to show them,
not to mention that it will give you a natural chemical lift.
Research shows that doing kindnesses to others gives us
a physiological high by releasing dopamine, our brain's
innate happiness drug. Studies show, for example, that
doing things like volunteer work can reduce depression,
lower anxiety, increase energy, alleviate physical ailments,
heighten feelings of self-worth, and extend life expectancy.

- **Donate blood.** See above.
- **Write a letter to someone.** It's easy to thank people and connect when we're feeling good, but more difficult to do so when we're feeling terrible. Which is why this has such a strong effect. I admit I have a strong bias toward this because so much of my life revolves around writing, but think about how you feel when you get an unexpected note from someone.

  At one point, during one of my worst days, I started to think about all the different people — friends, family, colleagues — who were trying to do good for me, by giving advice or sharing wisdom, offering practical help, lending an ear or a shoulder, or various other gestures, tangible and not. I wrote a group email thanking them all and assuring them that, even though I was going through a really dark and challenging period, their thoughtfulness and generosity gave me the faith that I could get through it and, over time, feel light and happy again. I didn't write this message to get anything back or because someone told me to or because it was something I was supposed to do. I found, after sending it, that I felt better. Happier, even, if only for that moment. Nothing had changed other than my having sent an email to a bunch of people. But it felt really good to do so. And that's because it feels good when we thank the people who are doing us a solid.

- **Talk to someone you wouldn't normally seek out.** For example: I'm an atheist, and I've long rejected synagogue and settings of religious worship. But during a period of particular confusion and dejection, I sought out one of the rabbis at the synagogue we'd attended as a family, not because he was a man of the cloth and I was hoping for miraculous inspiration from some Old Testament passage, but because I had always found him to be a person of great intelligence and sensitivity. In times of despair you could do worse than seek counsel from someone whose life mission is to always continue learning and helping others.

I wrote him a letter asking if he would grant me some time. He invited me to his home, and my chat with him there was one of the most important I had during the entire process. He gave no advice or direction. What he gave was a bigger gift than that: a heartfelt, deeply human conversation.

- **Buy fresh fruit.** Honest. There are three reasons. First, having natural stuff around helps because it's real. Second, fruits are sweet and juicy and nutritious and when you eat them, you can't help but feel a bit healthier and happier. Finally, they're colourful. I know I might sound a little bonkers to you at this point, but seriously, before you say no, go buy some apples, bananas, oranges, berries of any type, and mangoes or other tropical fruit, then display them on your kitchen countertop, and be honest, tell me if you don't feel a tick happier looking at them. Even more to the point, eat one of them, and then compare the feeling to scarfing a bag of chips or other classic emotional-eating staples, and tell me which makes you feel better.
- **Garden.** Getting your fingers dirty in the soil is a fabulous activity at any time, but especially when you're feeling down in the dumps. The explanation for it isn't actually so different from my previous point about buying fruit. The more you connect with natural things, the better you'll feel. That's why it feels good when you take the kids to a movie but great when you build a snow fort or sandcastle with them. If you have a garden, yard, lawn, or balcony, work directly with it — plant some flowers, mow, fertilize, water, till, prune, sculpt, place some rocks around the base of your tree if you have one, whatever. I know of few sensations that feel as purely good as working the land, even if it's just your little bit of land. And if you don't have a garden, yard, lawn, or balcony, take your green thumb inside: get a plant or

two if you don't have any, or if you already do, tend to them — give the leaves a nice bath with a soft cloth, get a nice planter, put in fresh soil. See if there is a community garden near you. I bet your kids would love helping tend a section of it together.

- **Decide to be positive.** I'm serious. It used to be assumed that positive experiences made us happy; we had no influence over our own state of mind. Current studies into the new discipline called Positive Psychology, along with cutting-edge research in neuroscience, tell a different story. We don't have to wait for good things to happen to get happy — we can get happy by deciding to be so.

  Here are three examples, described in the *The Happiness Advantage*, by Shawn Achor. One: a longitudinal study found that Catholic nuns whose diaries at age twenty had more joyful content lived longer than their contemporaries whose diaries contained less. Two: in another study, subjects assessed as happier beforehand recovered faster from an injected cold virus than those determined to be less happy. Three: doctors who were put in a positive mood before making a diagnosis showed almost three times more intelligence and creativity than doctors in a neutral mood, and made accurate diagnoses 19 percent faster. The lesson? While positive events can be the cause of happiness, they can also be the result.

- **Remember that you're never burdening someone who loves you.** I live in Toronto; Fulvia lives in Milan. There's a six-hour difference in our time zones. There were countless times when I was feeling low and the only thing in the world I wanted was to hear her voice or look into her eyes. But if it was, say, nine in the evening for me, that meant it was three in the morning for her. She would insist repeatedly that I call her at any hour, but at first I resisted doing so — she has a busy career, a home to manage, and, like me, three kids to raise. Eventually, I relented, and I'm glad

I did, because even a few minutes of being able to see or hear her soothed and centred me when nothing else could. Whether it's your new partner, your sibling, your parent, or your best friend, when someone who loves you tells you to call, call.

I've said several times that the process of transition is neither linear (it doesn't proceed along a straight, clean path) nor discrete (it doesn't happen in a vacuum). It goes in cycles, up and down, left and right, zagging when you expect it to zig. The same applies to your temperament and attitude. In even your lowest moments, not everything will feel sad, wrong, and miserable, and in your highest ones, not everything will feel good, happy, and right again. You're on a complicated journey containing multiple streams: practical, emotional, psychological, philosophical, and spiritual. Your kids are experiencing an even more complicated shift, because they've had less time to develop coping skills and perspective. They will advance and regress all the time, sometimes in ways that seem shocking and perplexing to you. Sometimes these swings will occur within the same day or hour.

As I said, I was really scared at first that I, and more importantly, my kids, might never feel light again. At first you're pretty much enveloped by the darkness, and, oh man, is it dark. But heed the words of author and childhood literacy advocate Greg Kincaid: "No matter how much falls on us, we keep plowing ahead. That's the only way to keep the roads clear." Stay positive within yourself, demonstrate empathy to your kids, continue being kind to others, and accept the unconditional caring and support of those who love you. All of these acts will help you understand this great challenge within the broader context of your life's journey. Eventually, you will feel the light start to come back, in pinpoints at first, then slivers, then big, broad rays.

———————

Ten Questions: My Workmate Thomas

What were the biggest mistakes you made with your kids during your split, and how have you addressed them?

I think my biggest mistake was my behaviour during drop-offs after weekends with my daughter. It's primarily the only time I see her mother face to face, and I've felt on many an occasion that I failed to remain emotionally calm, tolerant, forgiving, and loving toward her while my daughter is present. While this may be how I actually feel, and while I may experience physiological changes when seeing my ex — anxiety, fear, rising blood pressure — I know it's imperative I don't allow my child to see this, for a million different reasons.

Spirituality, meditation, and speakers on YouTube have been key in helping me recognizing my faults, and so every time I don't execute a "flawless" drop-off, for my daughter's sake and for my own sanity, I always analyze what happened, where might I have been at fault, what could I have done better. How did it impact my daughter? If it was something bad, what can I do in the future to ensure it doesn't happen again? Do I need to discuss it with her? She only gets to see her parents interact during these few minutes of her life every week, and she deserves to see them acting civil. Although there's nothing I can do about my ex's behaviour and can only control my own, it's a matter of ongoing personal growth.

Can you describe your lowest or hardest moments with your kids? How about moments when you saw light at the end of the tunnel?

I don't think I can really pinpoint any low moments after we split. The relationship had become fairly poor toward the end, and the split was more a relief followed by intense personal strength and growth as a father and human being. I really embraced the single-father thing until I met my new partner. I grew so much, so fast. I started my own side business, got into great shape, my career was going really well, I met an amazing woman who I've been with for two years and who is amazing with my daughter, and we're engaged and expecting a little one. It was like once I could stop walking on eggshells, I started dancing through life.

In your view, what do kids need most from their dad during or after a breakup?

I used to think the most important thing children needed from their parents was love, and after that, the practical necessities like food and water and a roof over their head. I've learned that the number-one thing children need is just to feel safe. When they feel that way, it opens up the gates for them to feel love, happiness, and warmth in life.

How much emotion did you show your kids with regard to your split? Where do you stand on how much "real" they should see versus how much they should be protected?

Well, again, I feel like it's really important to respect and honour my daughter's relationship with her mother, but if she's present while her mother is disrespectful to me, or if my ex acts inappropriately toward me, I do address the situation with her and talk about it to see how it made her feel. I'm an adult, I can take it. But what I think is important is to have that discussion in case she is feeling things she may have trouble understanding or managing, and help her navigate those feelings with love and guidance.

What would you say are the key hurdles to get over as a family before kids can start adjusting to the new normal?

I think my daughter is already pretty used to things. She has her life with her mom, and she has a very different life with me. I feel like she enjoys both, and that makes me happy for her.

How do you handle the practical issues of two households?

My ex has a tendency to dress our daughter in clothing that's too small, and steal the nice clothes we send her home in and send her back wearing junk clothes. She has also, on many occasions, kept toys that I sent home with her. At first it was frustrating. I am already paying child support and on top of that she is using me as a clothing and toy exchange, but as time went on I stopped caring. I would rather she steal from me and my child have new clothes that fit her and toys she enjoys. I now leave the gate open: whatever my daughter wants to bring back to her mother's, I allow. It's not my stuff, it's hers. She should be able to enjoy it as she pleases. In the end, it's just stuff. It comes down to my love for my daughter. I want the best for her. Always.

What are your top three pieces of advice to other dads for maintaining a loving and healthy relationship with their kids after a split?
First, show up. Be there when you say you will, do what you say you're going to, never make promises you don't intend to or can't keep, be interested in the things your children are interested in, and facilitate their interest in healthy things. Make sure your children always come first. Always.

Second, don't carry around emotions from the past. Everything happens for a reason. Everything right now in this very moment is exactly how it should be, so don't let negative emotions colour it. Don't let the beauty of the forest be ruined by one ugly tree.

Finally, do *your* best. As long as you do, and you know you're doing it, there is nothing you or anyone can say that would cause you to doubt yourself, because you know in your heart that you've done the best you can. That also applies to forgiving yourself. Sometimes, even when you do your best, you're going to fall short. Forgive yourself and move on. Have fun and love life. It's already short.

12

Exploring Your New Identity

The heart of a father is the masterpiece of nature.
— Antoine François Prévost d'Exiles

Not only has your family structure changed, but so has your status. Though you probably don't think much about it since your focus is on your kids, you're part of a new category: divorced dad. You're no different fundamentally, of course, and you'll find that most people, like your closest buddies, see you the same way as they did before. But certain contexts may alert you to the fact that you've joined a new group. The moms in the schoolyard, for example, seem to be looking at you differently — some not so kindly, others kind of extra kindly. Conversations with some people seem to carry a different, inquisitive tone. Male friends talk with vicarious enthusiasm about how much fun it must be to be "out there" again. Female friends tell you constantly about the women they want to set you up with, each of whom are, for all intents and purposes, flawless. The information flow with teachers, coaches, parents of your kids' friends, and anyone else involved in their lives is now more complicated because it occurs along two communication lines — to you and to your ex.

Sometimes, others' focus on the new category you've joined can prevent you from seeing that, as a result of the passage you've endured, you have become a new, better you. You have become not only a more self-aware and emotionally resourceful person, but also an even more committed and connected father. You've shown your kids lessons of patience, resilience, courage, and humanity they'll use throughout their lives, and you yourself have grown in ways you'll only come to understand later. As my friend Elliot says, "Don't expect to go back to being who you were before. You've grown. That guy is gone."

He's right. This is a new you, and with all the knowledge and experiences you're bringing into this new chapter, you're not "old you" or "married you" at all. What you are now is better you. This is because you know more about yourself as a person, a man, and a father. You know what you want in a relationship. You're less willing to compromise on things that are incompatible with who you are and what you value. Whether you were with your ex for three years or, like I was, fifteen, you've evolved as a human and come to a place in which you can explore different sides of yourself and give release to parts that may have been inhibited before.

The new identity you'll forge after your split is not composed of just your mental and physical self. It is also the new space you will create for you and your kids. You will have the opportunity to define a new environment in which all of you can thrive, bringing forward the best parts of your previous dynamic and establishing new rituals and traditions out of which special new memories will be formed. As you create your new space, both the physical look of it as well as its spirit and atmosphere, your kids will discover new colours and shades of themselves, just as you will. This combination — the tangible space and the feeling you create together within its walls — will allow all of you to enter a new dimension together. You are still you and they are still them, but entry into this new environment represents a crucial passage.

The new domain results largely from you doing things the way you'd like to do them, and your kids responding to the assertion of that independence. This isn't to say you were straitjacketed before, but the fact is, many of the men I've spoken to have told me that an essential part of their transition, and the one that seemed most transformative for their kids, lay in the opportunity to make their own decisions. I admit this was the case for me too, and I believe my kids have responded positively to the difference.

Again, the point of this is not to criticize my ex for disagreeing with my suggestions or exhibiting different habits or having different instincts about how to run a household. I'm not suggesting, either, that you should dwell on all the ways you feel your ex held you back or undermined you (even if you feel she did). The point is that one of the reasons relationships tend to become incompatible over time is because of the differences of opinion that arise between partners regarding how to coexist in, and co-manage, physical space. Some learn how to do it really well; others do it less and less well over time. Your own self-rediscovery will be strongly reflected in the pleasure you get from creating your own rules in your own space, and seeing your kids' positive responses to them.

Speaking of your space, let's touch on the domestic you versus the bachelor you. One part of your brain knows it's important to create a comfortable and welcoming home for the kids. However, another part may be tempted to revert to university-dorm-type habits like ordering pizza every night, leaving dishes piled in the sink, ignoring the colonies of dustballs collecting in the corners, leaving beds unmade and sheets unwashed for weeks at a stretch, and demonstrating general indifference to whether the place looks like a palace or a pigsty.

Forgive me for generalizing or making presumptions. I'm merely addressing a syndrome that Alyson Schafer calls "setting up a bachelor pad and not a home," by which she refers to the natural reflex one may have of reverting to an earlier stage even as you move into a new one. If you want to leave the toilet seat up as a statement of your new independence, go for it. But remember that kids benefit from structure and order, not disarray. A chaotic physical environment may cause them internal anxiety, not to mention that it sets a poor example for how they should tend to their own stuff and their own space now and later in life.

Sometimes, as Schafer suggests, this lack of attention can be a result of dads deciding the effort isn't worth it. "If the schedule dictates that the kids are with Dad a minority of the time," she says, "he may make the mistake of thinking, *They're mostly with her anyway, so I'm not going to make a big effort to make the place look like a home.* He doesn't think about decor, he doesn't put anything on the walls — he thinks, *Why should I go to the trouble, the kids aren't going to be here much anyway, and when they are here, they just want to be back home.*"

Whatever your custody schedule is, make your home wonderful. It will already be a fun place just by virtue of the fact that you're the captain of it, but make sure you also make it clean, organized, and cared for. Show the kids that you are invested in keeping it that way. They'll follow suit. Here are half-a-dozen-plus-one practical tips for making your new place one of domestic comfort, cleanliness, and enjoyment for you and your kids, and avoiding the accidental reversion to bachelorpadium.

- **Learn how to cook.** If you're not good at it already, use this as an opportunity to improve, so that you're not reliant on grilled cheese and PB&J. If you are already good at it, expand your horizons. Have your kids choose recipes and let them lead, with you as sous-chef. Make simple things, like soups and stews. Make semi-complicated things, like tuna casserole. Make sophisticated things, like lamb chops with balsamic reduction. Wake up on weekends and make smoothies and omelettes together. Don't rush meals or the preparation of them. Enjoy making a mess but do excellent cleanup. The kitchen is one of the best places to laugh, bond, explore, get creative, be silly, and achieve shared gratification in a job well done.
- **Get familiar with nice scents.** Again, I don't mean to stereotype you, but chances are you weren't the person in the relationship choosing the fragrant atomizers or scented mists. One way of showing your kids you care about the aesthetics of your home is to make it odoriferously pleasant. Slice up lemons and place them in a bowl at their bedsides.

Use rosemary, mint, and basil liberally. Get familiar with cedar blocks, aromatic sachets, and potpourri. Don't be intimidated by moisturizing creams and body oils. Want to know my kids' favourite thing about my place? Little candles. When I moved in, I bought a variety of them and told each of the kids to choose one for their bedroom. Dustin, Cory, and Alisha all now light a candle every night at bedtime and keep it at their bedsides to fall asleep to. Afterwards, I come in and blow the candles out one by one. It's a new tradition, shared within our new space together. Performing the ritual makes me cry just about every time. (Yes, a lot of stuff makes me cry. But these are good cries.)

- **Clean well and more often than you think you ought to.** Sweep constantly. Dust even more. Don't just wipe things — scrub them. Mop the kitchen floor on Sundays. (It's soothing.) Vacuum the floors and carpets. (Put on some music; I bet you'll be dancing in no time.) Don't ignore the inside of the oven or the fridge. Buy good sponges, cloths, wipes, and steel wool. Always have baking soda and vinegar handy, since that pairing can clean nearly anything on Earth.

- **Fluff and fold.** Take care of clothes properly — your kids' and your own. Fold shirts. Iron collars. Keep dressers and linen closets organized. Don't just take stuff out of the dryer and stuff it into drawers. Put T-shirts in attractive stacks. Steam your pants so the creases are sharp. Change bedsheets and pillowcases every week. If you're feeling bold, try to fold a fitted sheet. Don't neglect your bedroom at the expense of the kids' rooms. If they see that Daddy cares about his space, they'll care about theirs too.

- **Pay special attention to the bathrooms.** You have kids, after all, and kids are murder on bathrooms. Invest in good cleaning products for toilets, tubs, sinks, and mirrors. Buy rubber gloves and knee pads and use plenty of elbow grease. (Think of the workout!) Buy loofahs for the shower and an air pillow for the bath. Give your kids rewards for putting the cap back on the toothpaste, hanging towels after bathing, and, for the love of all that is good and pure, aiming for the bowl.

- **Learn how to fill your space without breaking the bank.** Homes don't need expensive things to look good. Most of the space on my walls is occupied by pictures of my kids contained in frames I got at Walmart. Shop around instead of making impulse buys. Take advantage of online selling and trading sites. Populate your space with the essentials first to make it feel like home — start with the kids' bedrooms — then work outward.

- **Get plants.** They produce oxygen. They look nice. They make you feel happy. It's fun to talk about and care for them together. Dustin has allergies that sometimes make it harder for him to sleep. I got a Peace Lily for his bedroom because it's a plant that helps clean the air. He sleeps better because of it. We just got another one called a Dracaena Dragon Jade Jewel for the living room. We nicknamed it "DDJJ."

If dads hear their kids refer to their ex's place as "home" often enough, they may overcompensate by trying to make *their* place Fun Central — go to bed when you want, play on screens for hours at a time, have ice cream for dinner and Pop-Tarts for breakfast, build forts with the furniture, don't worry about cleaning up. This might feel like the thing to do, but it won't actually help the kids get used to life in your new home. It's okay to feel like you want to relax the rules a bit compared with your previous environment, but you still need to be a parent. Psychotherapist Kyle Karalash looks deeper into this topic:

> I often wonder if the title of "fun parent" that seems so often applied to fathers is due not only to their desire to overcompensate with what they see as more desirable activities, but also to the stereotype that men are

less structured or capable of implementing rules. In my view, these assumptions are based on typical and unfair traditional thoughts of gender roles. Men are held up against these negative expectations, which we need to challenge. You can be loving and supportive and still enact curfews and routine. Take pride in your strengths and skills as a parent. The idea that men can only prove our affections and support through all play and no work needs to be deconstructed.

You have a sublime opportunity to interact with your kids in the same ways as before while at the same time creating a new set of memories, moments, and discoveries. And the more "complete" a parent you are within your space, the greater that opportunity. I'm not implying you weren't the whole package before, but some generalizations about gender roles hold up, and studies show that men do have a tendency to focus more on certain things (say, chasing the kids around while pretending to be a monster) than others (say, getting them to wash their hands). Now that you're the only parent in your space, you have a duty to your kids to play both roles: let them have whipped cream straight from the can for a laugh, but make sure they floss and brush after. They'll respect you a lot more for combining fun with rules than for being only Fun Dad or only Rules Dad.

Finally, involve your kids in the realization of the new environment. The number one way to make them feel that the new home is theirs is to make them part of its creation. I took my kids with me to see several apartments, asking their opinions and engaging them in conversations about how different spaces might be configured, always starting with their bedrooms. Once I found a place, I had each choose their own wall colours and furniture. Alisha loves showing off her room to friends and telling them she put together all the furniture. Yes, this makes me cry.

Do everything you can to communicate to your kids that this place is to be your home *together*, not Daddy's place where they sometimes stay. It will be strange for them at first to get used to the idea of having two homes, so it may be natural to hear them refer to your ex's place as "home" and your place as "Daddy's" for a bit. Don't take it personally. (I say this with a great deal of hypocrisy. It killed me every time my kids said it. But wise and caring people told me to be patient, and they were right, so I'm telling you the same.)

My anticipation of the kids' first night at my place was quickly doused by each of them experiencing different difficulties and anxieties about it. Change is hard, and the magnitude of this change was enormous for them, perhaps nearly the inverse of my feeling of excitement. I shouldn't have expected the transition to be simple, but I wanted so badly for them to be comfortable and happy there.

Fulvia had recently gone through the same transition with her three daughters, and reminded me of that indispensable nugget: look at it from the kids' perspective. She had created a warm and wonderful home for her girls, but they, too, had needed time to adjust. Her sweet compassion and soft wisdom helped me find the patience and faith I needed. Realizing when each of the kids felt comfortable in the new place was, when the time came, heartwarming. I remember how happy I was the first time I came home from work to find Cory and a few of his buddies hanging out at my place and playing video games. And I recall as clear as day the time I was speaking to Dustin on the phone, asking where he was. When he said, "I just got home" and I realized he was at my place, my heart soared. And the first time Alisha asked if she could have her birthday party at my place, I felt pure happiness. It takes time to create a new home and time for your kids to embrace it. But the result is worth the wait.

———————

There is, in many circles, an assumption that it's Mom who organizes everything, knows the schedule, and manages the kids' daily life, while Dad is unaware. Other parents, as well as teachers, coaches, relatives, babysitters, and people involved in your kids' lives may make this assumption, using your ex as a default point of contact in making plans, seeking or providing information, or requesting decisions. You may find yourself learning about things second-hand, or having conversations with people in which you get the sense that they assume you're somehow disconnected. I promise you this is a temporary phase. First, it will take time for you and your ex to establish a fluid dynamic whereby you communicate enough to be on top of things together. At first that communication will be like a branch going down a stream and getting diverted frequently, then dislodged again. Each week or month will be like another blockage being removed from the stream, until the waters are flowing freely (mostly).

The better the two of you get at co-parenting, the more comfortable others will become with you as a split couple. When you break up, the people around you don't necessarily know who they're supposed to talk to, for example, when they want to make plans for their kids with yours. They may not know your custody schedule. (*You* may not know your custody schedule.) They may not know whether, as a family, you want privacy for a while. They may not know whether you're getting along or are at war. Assert yourself, which will help those others around you and, in turn, your kids. Be proactive about contacting other parents for play dates. Establish the kind of dad you are so others know and can see it, and they'll respond accordingly.

In the first few months after my split, others would look at me strangely and act hesitant in our conversations. That was, I think, just a natural response to their not knowing how to act around me, or my ex, or us when they saw us together. Once they realized that I was still just normal me, they responded by being just normal them. Once again: as with every other aspect of your separation, the success of this part of the transition depends almost entirely on how you and your ex get along. If you make a snide comment about her every time you drop your kid off at a play date, do you think that parent is going to want to schedule another? If your children are always telling stories to their friends about how much you and your ex fight, do you think those friends' parents are going to consider your kids positive influences on them? Find a way to get along!

This also goes back to the importance of making your place a cozy and comfortable home rather than a bachelor pad. Parents of your kids' friends probably already know that you're a funny, smart, kind, generally awesome guy, but they know you as one half of a couple in the context of a shared home, and, fairly or not, they probably assume it was mostly your ex who maintained it. Naturally, they'll want to see whether you're also a responsible solo parent. They're not overtly judging you; they just want assurance about the kind of environment their kids are entering. Wouldn't you?

I think you'll find this process gratifying, because, while it's one thing to feel your own sense of joy in moving on, in a way it's even cooler to receive the acknowledgement and confirmation from people around you that this new chapter exists, and that they're happy to be part of it.

Which leads me to the friends thing. Yes, there are times when former couple friends of yours are forced to "choose" one of you. A common example concerns family events. Say the son of a couple you met together and were "equal" friends with is having — to use a frequent example from my own life — a bar mitzvah. Obviously it would be weird for them to invite both you and your ex. Don't be offended when they "choose" your ex as the parent to invite. I'm putting "choose" in quotes because I want you to put yourself in their shoes. The perception that friends are making these "choices" is unfair. It isn't as though they're rating your respective characters; they're just having to decide whose name goes on the invitation.

Don't fall into the trap of saying, "They're choosing her over me." First, people have their own stuff to deal with. They aren't likely spending hours talking about you and your ex. Second, sometimes they're just going to have to decide who fits into certain logistics. Don't blame them. It isn't any easier for them than it is for you. Also, I encourage you to resist the urge to get people to "believe your side of the story." Your close friends will naturally take your "side," and your ex's friends will naturally take hers. But the one thing they all want is the best for your kids, and for you as a family. Those who care about you will be most interested in making sure you're okay, as opposed to listening to you gripe.

Some people may make private judgments of you. Some may laud you for your courage, while others may stigmatize you for your cruelty. But you have not one iota of influence over the opinions of others, so don't sweat it. Plus, no matter what others may assume, the only two people who know the real story are you and your ex. What's important is your relationship with your kids and figuring out how to move forward as a family.

———————

Just as you have a new status, your kids have a new status by association. Everything that affects you as part of the new category you've entered as a single dad affects them too. My advice is not to hide the split in front of them. If you act cagey and embarrassed about the situation, they will feel ashamed as well. I'm not saying you should go around wearing an "I got divorced" T-shirt, but don't shy away from the fact, either. Though this change really hurts, the sooner you can make it real for your kids, the sooner they can start to adapt to it.

My kids responded best when I acknowledged the split, as well as its difficulty, to others. If I saw a friend for the first time after public news of our family breakup, and the friend expressed condolences, I think my kids preferred it when I said something like, "It's really tough on all of us right now, but the kids are being their amazing selves and we're doing our best to get through it a step at a time," instead of lowering my head, changing the topic, or shooing the kids into another room. It may sound strange for me to encourage you to make your kids part of conversations about such a painful event in their lives, but the sooner this change can become part of reality for them, the sooner they can start to feel like they're okay because, hey, Daddy's there talking to what's-his-name about the fact that he and Mommy broke up, but what's-his-name seems to be cool with it, and the sun still came up today, and everything else is kind of the same, so maybe things aren't as bad as they seem.

I don't mean to make reality sound so simple — it isn't — but I do mean to say that your kids feel like the jigsaw puzzle of their lives has been broken apart, and every moment that can represent "okayness" to them is like a piece of that puzzle being put back into place. If you make the breakup seem like a big, bad secret, it's going to feel that way to them too. If you bring it sensitively into the light, you will help them understand that, even though a catastrophe happened, it can be managed, and that their new identity, and that of your family, is not bad, just different.

The last thing I want to say about the new you is that, even while you emerge happily into this new phase, make sure your kids continue to be able to recognize you as the anchor they've always had. Some things will remain the same — the inside you, your closest friends, your values and beliefs, the way you laugh, your sneeze, your list of favourite comedies. But there will be many changes in you too. After a split, you're inevitably reborn. The circumstances of your life change, and you change with them. You'll discover new interests, do new things. You'll tap into parts of yourself that were dormant or non-existent before. You'll gain greater self-awareness and a different level of confidence to go with it.

Yes, you're like the proverbial butterfly having emerged from its cocoon. (Actually, that's not quite accurate. It's more like you've been through a medieval gauntlet, or one of those cartoon machines that shake and rattle violently until you get ejected out the other side.) But remember that what your kids need most during this time is consistency. Make sure they know that their dad from before is the same as their dad now.

The parts of the new you that you feel most energized about may be the same things that prove unnerving to your kids. You may feel like a new person and a dad who can have true quality time with his kids and be his real self around them. And they will benefit in lots of ways from this you that emerges from the wreckage. However, a you they don't recognize can be scary. The best thing they can see is a new version of the same you — a happier, lighter, more real version. Good: Dad has taken up swimming and does laps every morning. Not so good: Dad has taken up the lambada and is going to clubs three nights a week. Good: Dad is working really hard on his new business, but still puts the computer and phone away whenever he's with us. Not so good: Dad's got some new venture we don't really understand because he doesn't talk to us about it, and even when we're with him, we don't really spend time together.

Be the same loving, caring, and devoted dad they've always known even as you undergo what is a certain, and positive, metamorphosis. Comedian Mike Myers said, "Anyone who tells you fatherhood is the greatest thing that can happen to you, they are understating it." I feel the same, and I know you do too. Everything you're going through now will serve its purpose later. Face this trial with poise and serenity, and be your best self in every moment you can. Above all, let your kids know that your most important role is Dad, and always will be. I wish you and your family the very best.

Acknowledgements

I am indebted to the numerous fathers who took time to share with me not only their stories but also their feelings. Only some of these were men I already knew. Others were friends of friends; still others, dads who simply heard about the book and wanted to add their part in the shared hope of helping others. If this book allows even one father to make the passage through divorce with a little less pain, I will consider it a success.

I am grateful to the many professionals who generously paused their schedules to answer my questions and offer insights to help dads move forward through sometimes crushing grief and sadness. I am appreciative of these experts both for the consistent themes they raised as a group and the specific views each of them provided to help shine light on the subject from different angles.

I am thankful to the team at Dundurn for sharing my belief in the potential value of this book, understanding my reasons for writing it, and making me feel like part of their wonderful publishing family from day one. Any author would be fortunate to work with a group of people so professional, knowledgeable, and unified in purpose.

I am blessed to have a family who provides unlimited encouragement and support, and who always makes me feel that what I do is worthwhile. From the earliest days my mother, father, and sister gave me the confidence to believe that my desire to write made sense, challenged me to do it as well as I could, and celebrated every piece that had my name under it.

I am forever thankful to my partner, Fulvia. She is a person of steadfast character and intelligence, a woman of deep compassion and kindness, and a partner of infinite caring and devotion, who has sustained me through countless moments and supported this book from conception to fruition. Because of her I am a better father and a better man.

BOOK CREDITS

Developmental Editor: Dominic Farrell
Project Editor: Jenny McWha
Copy Editor: Naomi Pauls
Proofreader: Megan Beadle

Cover Designer: Matthew Maaskant
Interior Designer: Courtney Horner

Publicist: Elham Ali

DUNDURN

Publisher: J. Kirk Howard
Vice-President: Carl A. Brand
Editorial Director: Kathryn Lane
Artistic Director: Laura Boyle
Production Manager: Rudi Garcia
Director of Sales and Marketing: Synora Van Drine
Publicity Manager: Michelle Melski
Manager, Accounting and Technical Services: Livio Copetti

Editorial:
Allison Hirst, Dominic Farrell, Jenny McWha, Rachel Spence, Elena Radic, Melissa Kawaguchi

Marketing and Publicity:
Kendra Martin, Kathryn Bassett, Elham Ali, Tabassum Siddiqui, Heather McLeod

Design and Production:
Sophie Paas-Lang